Stories of TRUE FINANCIAL FREEDOM

Crown's Money Map in Real Lives

Introduction by

HOWARD DAYTON

Bridge-Logos

Orlando, Florida 32822

Bridge-Logos

Orlando, FL 32822 USA

Stories of True Financial Freedom
by Crown Financial Ministries

Library of Congress Catalog Card Number: 2006926539
International Standard Book Number 0-88270-115-0

G163.316.N.m606.35250

Contents

Introduction

THROUGHOUT THE AGES, God has used true stories to permanently record His unique work in people's lives. The hallmark signature of His presence is a changed life. And He is infinitely creative in the way He accomplishes His purposes.

A friend once introduced his personal story like this: "I am about to share with you my own testimony. It is a true account of what God has done in my life. However, it is not a promise or guarantee of what God will do in yours. You should listen to my story and be encouraged by the faithfulness of God and the awesomeness of His mysterious ways to intercede in our daily affairs." What a great context for the stories you will read in this book!

The Scriptures declare that God is faithful. A verse I particularly like says, "And God, who called you into fellowship with his Son, Jesus Christ, is faithful."[1] The entire Bible demonstrates that God always keeps His promises. The unpredictable part is how and when He will keep them—His means of delivery. Consider these examples.

• Two unlikely caregivers, ravens and a starving widow, were both used by God to provide for Elijah.[2] I think this qualifies as a unique delivery system.

• The Lord filled another widow's jars with oil so she could pay her debts and have resources to survive. Her creditors were attempting to collect her children as payment on her debt when the provision was uniquely delivered.[3]

• When tax collectors came to Jesus, He gave Peter specific directions to catch a fish in whose mouth would be a coin worth the exact amount of the taxes due. Jesus used the occasion to demonstrate His authority through this unique, just-in-time delivery.[4]

The stories you will read in this book are stories of God's unwavering faithfulness and His mysterious ways of interceding in our daily affairs. *Stories of True Financial Freedom* include profiles of a young girl whose beloved horse was struck by lightning, of a married couple whose marriage was quickly jeopardized by financial stress, of a husband and father who sought the Lord for a dramatic career change, of a heartbroken family faced with overwhelming medical expenses, of a dairy farmer who staved off bankruptcy against the advice of his lawyers. These testimonies will stir your heart and move you to seek God's will for your own life. The Lord Jesus Christ always does His part. Our part is to completely trust Him regardless of the unique circumstances that surround us.

God's Word provides us with a complete roadmap for our financial needs. Most people know that the Bible says something about ten percent of their income. What many of them do not realize, however, is that it gives significant direction regarding 100 percent. In the Bible's 2,350-plus verses relating to money and possessions, we find principles that help us earn, save, spend wisely, give generously, maintain integrity, get out of debt, experience contentment, develop an eternal perspective, and teach our children to do the same. As my son likes to say, "Dad, the Bible covers the whole enchilada." I want to be sure you understand five key biblical principles for gaining true financial freedom.

KEY PRINCIPLE ONE: **God owns everything.** The Bible tells us, "The earth is the Lord's and everything in it."[5]

KEY PRINCIPLE TWO: **We are to be faithful managers of all God entrusts to us.** "It is required in stewards that a man be found faithful."[6]

KEY PRINCIPLE THREE: **We must recognize and yield to God's control of our finances.** David prayed, "We adore you [Lord] as being in control of everything."[7]

KEY PRINCIPLE FOUR: **Faithfulness with money requires self-control, and God provides it.** "But the fruit of the Spirit is love, joy, peace, patience, kindness, goodness, faithfulness, gentleness and self-control."[8]

KEY PRINCIPLE FIVE: **Celebrate each step as you make steady progress.** "They will celebrate your abundant goodness and joyfully sing of your righteousness."[9]

As you read these compelling testimonies, I pray that God will move your heart to live totally by His financial principles. That is why we developed the *Crown Money Map.*™ It is a simple, step-by-step guide to true financial freedom. Regardless of where you may be on your journey, it is never too soon or too late to begin to manage money God's way. I cannot encourage you enough to take the next steps and let us help you. To learn more about the *Crown Money Map*™ and to purchase a copy, go to Crown.org/MoneyMap. While you're there, take a moment to explore some of the other valuable resources available at Crown.org.

Finally, let me share with you some of my own story. The turning point of my life came in 1971. I started attending a weekly breakfast with several young businessmen and was impressed by their energy and business savvy. But more than that, I was attracted to the quality of their lives. I didn't know what they had, but whatever it was, I wanted it.

I was part owner of a successful restaurant, had married my wonderful wife, and we lived in a comfortable home. I had everything I thought would give me happiness and a sense of accomplishment, but felt neither. Something was missing.

I was surprised to hear these men speak openly of their faith in God. I grew up going to church, but it meant nothing to me. A friend described how I could enter into a personal relationship with Jesus Christ, explaining five truths from the Bible I had never understood before.

1. God loves you.

He wants you to know Him and experience a meaningful life. God desires an intimate relationship with each of us. *"For God so loved the world, that He gave His only begotten Son, that whoever believes in Him should not perish, but have eternal life"* (John 3:16). *"I [Jesus] came that they might have life, and have it abundantly"* (John 10:10).

2. Unfortunately, we are separated from God.

God is holy—which means God is perfect, and He cannot have a relationship with anyone who is not perfect. My friend asked if I had ever sinned—done anything that would disqualify me from perfection. "Many times," I admitted. He explained that every person has sinned, and that the consequence of sin is separation from God. *"For all have sinned and fall short of the glory of God"* (Romans 3:23). *"Your sins have cut you off from God"* (Isaiah 59:2, NLT).

This diagram illustrates our separation from God:

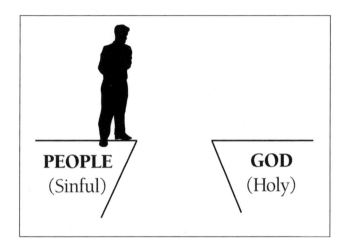

PEOPLE
(Sinful)

GOD
(Holy)

An enormous gap separates us from God. Individuals try without success to bridge this gap through their own efforts, such as philosophy, religion, or living a good moral life.

3. God's only provision to bridge this gap is Jesus Christ. Jesus Christ died on the cross to pay the debt for our sin. Colossians 2:13-14 says it this way, "[God] *made you alive together with* [Christ], *having forgiven us all our transgressions, having cancelled out the certificate of debt ... having nailed it to the cross."*

Christ bridged the gap between God and people. *"Jesus said... 'I am the way, and the truth, and the life; no one comes to the Father but through Me'"* (John 14:6*). "God demonstrates*

His own love towards us, in that while we were yet sinners, Christ died for us" (Romans 5:8). Someone described this in these terms: We had a debt we could not pay; Jesus paid this debt that He did not owe.

This diagram illustrates our union with God through Jesus Christ:

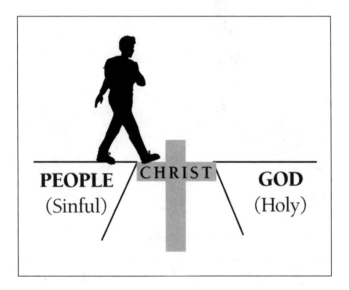

4. This relationship is a gift from God.

My friend explained that by an act of faith I could receive the free gift of a relationship with God. The transaction appeared totally inequitable. I had learned in business that any time two people were convinced they were getting more than they were giving up, you had a transaction. But now I was being offered a relationship with God, and it was a free gift! *"For by grace you have been saved through faith; and that not of yourselves, it is the gift of God; not as a result of works, so that no one may boast"* (Ephesians 2:8-9).

5. We must each receive Jesus Christ individually.
I had only to ask Jesus Christ to come into my life to be my Savior and Lord. So I did! As my friends will tell you, I am a very practical person—if something does not work, I stop doing it quickly. I can tell you from more than 30 years of experience that a relationship with the living God works. And it is available to you through Jesus Christ. Nothing in life compares with the privilege of knowing Christ personally. We can experience true peace, joy, and hope when we know Him.

If you desire to know the Lord and are not certain whether you have this relationship, I encourage you to receive Jesus Christ right now. Pray a prayer similar to this suggested one: "Father God, I need you. I invite Jesus to come into my life as my Savior and Lord and make me the person you want me to be. Thank you for forgiving my sins and giving me the gift of eternal life."

If you asked Christ into your life, congratulations! You have made the most important decision anyone could ever make. Expect God to become active in your life in a way you've never seen before, and make sure you cooperate with Him.

After praying that prayer, Bev and I committed to be "ruthlessly faithful" to living by God's financial principles. When we started, we were tens of thousands of dollars in debt, had little savings, and were not generous givers. Our attitudes about money and our spending habits strained our marriage terribly.

We wanted to work toward true financial freedom—to get in a position where we didn't need to earn a salary to meet our needs. We wanted to be able to volunteer all or part of our time to serve our church or a ministry without having to receive a wage if the Lord wanted us there.

As great as that goal was, it seemed unrealistic, and we had all kinds of obstacles and questions. Where should we start? What should we do next? How could we stay motivated for so long? Were we just dreaming? These challenges were compounded because our finances were in such poor shape.

We knew this would take a long time and require a lot of effort, but that it was possible by God's grace. About that time, I stumbled across the "steady plodding" principle. Proverbs 21:5 says, *"Steady plodding brings prosperity…"* (TLB). The original Hebrew words for *"steady plodding"* picture a person filling a large barrel one handful at a time. Little by little the barrel is filled to overflowing.

This was the way we could reach true financial freedom. We needed to have a plan with a series of small, achievable steps along the way. Then we needed to prioritize those steps according to God's way of handling money. And finally, we always needed to focus on accomplishing the next step on the journey no matter what challenges we faced.

We lived what has become the *Crown Money Map.*™ And it works! We have experienced true financial freedom, and for the past 20 years I have served as a full-time volunteer at Crown Financial Ministries.

Today, our vision at Crown is "to see the followers of Christ in every nation faithfully living by God's financial principles in every area of their lives." And because you are reading this book, you are one of those we have been praying for to begin that journey today. Please let us know how you are doing and how we can serve you. May the Lord Jesus Himself richly bless you as you faithfully serve Him.

Howard Dayton
Cofounder and CEO
Crown Financial Ministries

Endnotes

1 I Corinthians 1:9 NIV
2 I Kings 17
3 II Kings 4
4 Matthew 17:24-26
5 Psalm 24:1 NIV
6 I Corinthians 4:2 NIV
7 I Chronicles 29:11 TLB
8 Galatians 5:22 NIV
9 Psalm 145:7 NIV

God and Money:

The Journey of Sharla Bickley

By Margaux Stuart

SHARLA BICKLEY was working as a petroleum engineer on an oil rig in Peru when she sensed a passion to do more with her life. Through the study of Scripture in her Crown small group, Bickley learned the meaning of contentment and left her career in the oil industry to commit to full-time ministry.

As director of Christian Service and Membership at Highland Park Presbyterian Church (HPPC), Bickley now guides people who, like herself, desire to serve the Lord with their gifts and passions.

The youngest of four children, Bickley, 40, grew up in Shreveport, Louisiana, and graduated from Louisiana State

University with a degree in petroleum engineering. She spent most of her adult life traveling across the country and around the world, both with the oil industry and on her own. Five years ago, Bickley was living in Washington, D.C. when she recommitted her life to Christ. As Bickley grew in her faith, she began to see God's plan for her life unfold.

"I left Capitol Hill when I was recruited by Mobil and moved to Dallas into an international drilling and engineering job," Bickley said. She believes God had reasons to place her in Dallas. For one, she found a "strong support system" at Highland Park.

"I was still traveling and spending a lot of time in remote locations, on a rig, with a bunch of guys, not one Christian among them," Bickley said of her Dallas-based engineering career. Bickley said as she "struggled with how to thrive in that kind of environment," Highland Park provided a strong foundation to her spiritual growth.

"I went through a spiritual gifts class at HPPC," Bickley said, and found her interests "were definitely in the stewardship area." HPPC uses the class to help members analyze their personality types and find out how they can best serve the Lord. The course opened her eyes to the gift of giving, she said.

Shortly thereafter, Bickley signed up for the Crown study, which became a life-changing catalyst. Through Crown, Bickley realized God's part in her finances, and after assessing her savings, she made a decision to leave the oil industry.

"After taking the Crown class, I recognized for the first time that what I had put away was enough, and I didn't have to keep working," she said. Although Bickley had always handled her money conservatively and responsibly, the Scriptural focus of Crown gave her a new perspective.

"The point of life was always to work hard to save money for the future," said Bickley of her mindset before Crown. "A successful career was defined by having a good salary and managing it correctly. I just didn't relate that to God."

Bickley said her previous understanding of God and finances, which had been "just to tithe," changed greatly in the area of giving. Although she had been tithing for more than a year before Crown, it was not until she completed the study that Bickley experienced the blessing of giving.

Bickley recalled one instance on an assignment in South America: She made a giving decision on a Friday and was told the following Monday what her bonus would be for completing the assignment. Her bonus was identical to the amount she had given away three days before.

Bickley now operates with the understanding that it "all belongs to God." Even today, she said, "On my TV at home, I still have the 'property of God' labels that I made three years ago." Bickley used the labels to remind herself of the biblical principle of God's ownership of everything. "I'm a very visual learner. It took giving it all to Him and recognizing through that that I was content."

Experiencing contentment is what finally led Bickley into the ministry. Serving as director of Christian service and membership at Highland Park, Bickley rejoices in God's perfect plan. Her life, Bickley said, "was purely put in place, and when I look back it's miraculous to me that I landed in Dallas, at this church, with this job."

No longer on the move, Bickley is excited about her new life in Dallas. "I bought my first house on a 'church mouse' salary," she said with a smile, "and all I want to do is stay home and garden. The wanderlust is gone."

Bickley may be "settled" by her standards, but the passion with which she serves the Lord shows no sign of settling down. Ever the engineer, Bickley has introduced new tools and processes to her department, and has integrated the spiritual gifts inventory into every new member class at HPPC. She also directs many congregants to the Crown study.

"I try to explain that [Crown] is a much broader experience than just looking at your wallet," Bickley said. "Every issue Crown covers affects your whole life."

When sharing her own Crown experience, Bickley said her career shift into full-time ministry is "a little scary for some people to hear. I tell them that their world's going to rock."

When Bickley encourages people to sign up for Crown or to take a spiritual gifts inventory, she does so with the confidence that their lives will be affected, just as hers was. Bickley is grateful to be serving in the same ministry position that had such an impact on her life.

"I walk in every day and say, 'OK, God, this is your ministry, and I'm here for you,'" Bickley said. In a drastically different environment from the oil rigs of South America, Bickley looks at work through a different lens. She describes the humbling experience of remembering that her office has a steeple on it and needing to walk in that respect.

Even with a two-thirds cut in pay and the weighty responsibility of guiding new members in the church, Bickley said she has no doubt that she is right where God wants her to be.

"I think fondly of the opportunities I've had to see the world and go places, but I do not want to go back," she said. "I do not miss it. I don't miss one second of it. I've never felt so solid."

In Philippians 4:7, Paul speaks of the *"peace of God, which surpasses all comprehension"* (NASB). That peace radiates from Bickley's countenance and speech. Giving thanks to God, she states with confidence, "I am doing what I want to be remembered for."

Sign Post

Life is more than working and saving money for the future. Learning that all belongs to God and what your spiritual gift is brings true contentment.

"He who has been stealing must steal no longer, but must work, doing something useful with his own hands, that he may have something to share with those in need" (Ephesians 4:28).

Bouncing Back:

Charlie and Julia Sizemore

By Margaux Stuart

SUCCESS IN THE BUSINESS WORLD does not always translate to success in one's personal finances, many students of Crown Financial Ministries have learned.

Charlie and Julia Sizemore, whose family is well on its way to getting out of debt after years of relying on credit cards, realized that truth in their first Crown study.

"I've got an engineering degree and a masters in business," Charlie said. "For years I've been in control of and responsible for multimillion-dollar operations, and I could do it well. But I didn't have the slightest clue of how to run a household.

"That was what was frustrating on my end. I could nail a million-dollar budget within 2 percent, but I could not get within 15 percent of a home budget."

Charlie's 20-plus-year career as a petroleum engineer has been a rocky road for him, his wife Julia, and their two teenage daughters, Lindsay and Kristen.

He entered Texas Tech University during the Texas oil boom of the 1970s, when significant financial benefits were assured to recent petroleum engineering grads.

Three years later, right before he graduated, the oil boom had become an oil bust, and Charlie's career since has been marked by multiple layoffs, withdrawals from the Texas Employment Commission, long-distance commuting, and relocating.

Julia nodded with a smile. "The wives have a joke. It's not 'Has your husband been laid off?' but 'How many times has your husband been laid off?' "

Like many of his coworkers, Charlie and his family weathered the bad times by depending on credit cards.

"When the oil industry was down, we used our credit cards quite a bit; we didn't even think about it. We just kept using them and using them and realized we had incurred a tremendous amount of debt," Charlie said.

The family's attitudes toward money would change as drastically as their surroundings when Charlie's latest job change took them across the state of Texas, from the small city of Midland to the outskirts of Dallas.

Julia recalled the billboard that introduced them to Crown Financial Ministries.

"We were driving down Loop-820 and saw on the billboard of Richland Hills Church, 'Want to find out what God has to say about your money?' "

When she and Charlie attended the church service that Sunday, Julia pointed to the Crown announcement in the bulletin and told her husband, "This is why we're here."

One Crown small group and two years later, the Sizemores have reduced their debt by 30 percent, Julia is running her own Web design business, and the whole family has benefited from a shared responsibility in their finances.

"It's opened up a lot of lines of communication, because all four of us are more aware of where we are financially," Julia said. "Now we all sit down, and if there's a need we look at the need; or if there's something that we want we start saving for that."

The Sizemores saw more stability in their lives when they gave God a bigger role in their career and personal financial decisions.

Living by God's provision has alleviated many sleepless nights for Charlie, who had always worried about the future. He'd like to help others find that same sense of peace about their finances.

"As the market is failing and with the dot-com fallout, you see the same thing as the 70s oil boom: a lot of people became extremely successful because they happened to be in the right place at the right time [but] had no spiritual foundation," Charlie said. "And things went sour because they didn't have that grounding. It's so easy to get caught up in the game and lose your priorities."

Charlie is eager to help people cope with financial stress because he knows what debt and unemployment feel like. He now serves as a volunteer budget counselor through Crown.

"I primarily want to work with young couples to keep them from making the mistakes I made," Charlie said. "It never would have occurred to me, 22 years old with a college degree, that I needed to look to the Bible for financial advice."

For Charlie's family, changing bad spending habits did not come easily; it took both commitment and the grace of God.

"If we had not had Crown, we'd still be ignoring [our debt]," he said. "It took us 10 years to get there, and we've been working on it solid for three years now. ... I think the first six months you're just changing habits. It's kind of like putting the brakes on and then you start moving backward."

Julia said they plan to be credit card free in three years and completely debt-free in 10 years. As they make steady progress, they are encouraged by God's blessings.

"If you're faithful with what you're doing, God takes care of you," Julia said. "Periodically, God sends us little checks. ... We'll get a refund [that] matches exactly where we need to be in our budget."

Like her husband, Julia wants to share her wisdom with others. She serves on the DFW Crown City Team and has led the Crown Teen Study. Having applied the principles she learned in Crown to her own Web design business, Julia is leading a group of business women through Larry Burkett's study, *Business by the Book*. She is starting her company slowly, without accumulating debt, and donating her services to ministries.

In addition to finding more ways to serve, the Sizemores also have experienced the joy of giving. "Even though we are still on a very strict budget, we've been able to give more money than we've ever been able to give, and I've really enjoyed that," Julia said.

Charlie and Julia have already begun instructing their daughters in godly stewardship. For example, they required Lindsay and Kristen to take the Crown study before opening checking accounts, and they expect their daughters to print out budgets and balance checkbooks. Julia does not want her children to learn financial discipline the hard way.

"We've been through some very interesting times," she said. "But when you put it all in perspective, and you turn to God, you know that it's all okay. When you look back, God knew exactly what He was doing."

Sign Post

Business financial success does not mean personal financial success. It is easy to get caught up in "The Game" and lose your priorities. The truth of the Bible brings change when we do what it says.

"His master replied, 'Well done, good and faithful servant! You have been faithful with a few things; I will put you in charge of many things. Come and share your master's happiness!'" (Matthew 25:23).

Back to School:

Corporation to Coach

By Ken Gossage and Chuck Thompson

KEN GOSSAGE had a lot at stake. Educated as an engineer, he'd worked 17 years for the same company. He'd spent the last seven of those years as manager of a manufacturing/ distribution plant. Now, his employer, a medium-sized private company, was being swallowed by a big fish—a public corporation that was 10 times larger. To preserve the gains he'd made, he had to impress his new bosses.

Although Ken had grown frustrated with the corporate world, it had provided his family with a comfortable lifestyle. But as a Christian, he knew that God sometimes makes drastic changes in the lives of His children to shake them out of their comfort zones and move them to total dependence on Him.

Ken and his wife, Dede, began praying, and some friends from Crown in their hometown of Gainesville, Georgia introduced them to the ministry's Career Direct® assessment.

"I had planned my own career path in college without considering that God had designed me for His purposes and

might have a more fulfilling career in mind," Ken says. "Interestingly, the best match recommended by the assessment was to teach high school and coach."

Ken had enjoyed coaching when his children were younger, but the obstacle of living off a teacher's salary seemed too great for him to overcome. So, for the next three years he threw himself into his job.

Changes at work

"Trying to impress the new leadership and prove I was where God wanted me to be, I became entangled in the bureaucracy and politics of the giant corporation," he says.

But as Ken worked harder, he seemed to have less influence on the people and decisions around him. Disillusioned and exhausted, he had to make sense of his life, so he asked God for answers.

At this point, some unexplainable events and opportunities came along. "They were not all positive," Ken says, "but through my renewed eyes of faith, they had the unmistakable imprint of God."

On the negative side, Ken's vice president, to whom he had reported since he joined the company fresh out of college, was fired. The VP had worked for the company 25 years.

On the positive side, Ken received some unsolicited information about a unique teacher certification program.

Then, a complete stranger to Ken's division of the company was hired to replace his former VP. Within a few months, the new boss shook up the management structure so much that Ken was left with a nice salary but very little responsibility.

"I sensed that God was trying to literally push me out the door," he says. "He had tried discouragement and weariness, and now, on top of all that, boredom. Remembering the counsel I had received from the assessment, I took a small step of faith and applied to the master's degree/certification program that had mysteriously appeared in the mail."

During the next few months, it seemed that each step of faith resulted in an open door for Ken. He was one of 10 people accepted into the very selective certification program.

And with his undergraduate engineering degree, he would need only 48 hours (four semesters) to graduate.

Next, he had to unveil his education plan to his new boss and seek that person's approval, which seemed impossible. Instead, the boss replied, "No problem. You let me know what hours you'll work each semester, and when you need to leave permanently, we'll start you on severance pay for six months."

Still, Ken and Dede had to wrestle with the issue of how they would live on a teacher's salary, and the following months were stressful for both of them as they considered future expenses like college for two teenage children.

Changes at home

In an effort to avoid conflict with Dede, Ken had limited communication with her about his plans. "If I could do it all over again, I would discuss my plans with her," he says. "Husbands and wives are supposed to be one. A man needs the support of his wife, and she needs to know what he's doing."

With the burden of working 35 to 40 hours per week and spending 15 hours per week in school, Ken needed help from somewhere, and he spent much of his free time talking to the Lord and getting assurance from Him.

From left to right: Walker, Dede, Daphne, and Ken Gossage.

When Ken first shared his education plans with Dede, her initial reaction was that "he should go and pray about it some more." She was a stay-at-home mom and had a part-time business, which allowed her a lot of flexibility. If Ken became a teacher, she knew her lifestyle would have to change.

In the months that followed, both of them came to a place of brokenness, but Dede was confident that, in time, they would work it out. "I think God wanted to teach us a new level of trust," she says. "I probably suffered from a 'rights' mentality. I laid that down and forced myself to do things for Ken that I knew he would appreciate. This added to the healing process."

Dede worked part-time as an interior decorator, and when Ken got a teaching job, she and her daughter, Daphne, decorated his class. This allowed her to be a part of his world. She also attended his high school football games, even though she had never been a football fan. "It's a lot of fun," she says, "especially when you're winning."

A change for the better

Ken left the company where he had been employed 20 years and began student teaching in January 2000. He drew his severance pay, which expired exactly when he received his first paycheck as a teacher. In July 2003, Ken's former employer announced that in September it would close the plant he had managed.

As a math teacher, Ken was in high demand and received several teaching offers, but he was drawn to a small public school in Buford, Georgia.

His coaching duties at Buford include football and junior varsity baseball, and in the three years he has been at the school, the football team has played in three state championship games.

It has won the state championship the last two years and had a winning streak of 30 straight games going into the fall 2003 season.

"During my first three years, I have experienced what most coaches or teachers never experience in a lifetime," Ken says. "Now that's a rewarding job!"

But beyond coaching and teaching, God has blessed Ken and Dede financially. In the past they tithed and gave to ministries, and their only debt was their mortgage, but they still seemed to live month to month and had limited savings.

Although Ken made less than half of his previous income in his first year of teaching, he and Dede never noticed the change. The second year she went to work at Crown, and although their income was only 80 percent of what it had been in previous years, they were able to increase their giving and finish the year with $10,000 in savings, which was a big help with their children's college expenses.

Ken says, "During my first three years, I have experienced what most coaches or teachers never experience in a lifetime."

"Our giving has stayed the same, and we finished my third year of teaching with more than $10,000 in savings," Ken says. "As a mathematician, it makes no sense, but as a Christian, I know God has blessed our lives."

Sign Post

 Life plans can change when one encounters the will of God, which He has designed into each individual. God wants to free us from the entanglements of the world's systems. Open communications with your spouse can allow God to work His perfect plan.

"There is a way that seems right to a man, but in the end it leads to death" (Proverbs 16:25).

Maxmimzing their Means:
Steve and Annette Economides

ANNETTE AND STEVE ECONOMIDES (economy-dis) have been called some pretty unsavory names: "cheapskates," "tightwads," "penny pinchers." But names don't bother this economizing couple from Scottsdale, Arizona. They've found the secret to contentment, and they're not keeping it to themselves.

Instead, they're focused on their calling to help other families make the most of their money and their lives.

Their frugal trek started before they were married. In 1981, in a marriage prep class at their church, they were required to read Larry Burkett's book, *Your Finances in Changing Times*.

They started their marriage with a budget in place and no debt. Together, they have applied God's financial principles to every purchase and decision. That application has included shopping at thrift stores and consignment shops, doing their own haircuts, and borrowing free movies from the local library.

When Steve and Annette were newly married, they had no idea of the fantastic journey that the Lord had planned for them. By their first wedding anniversary, their family had

Steve and Annette Economides and their five children.

grown to three. Steve earned $7 an hour as a graphic designer. Annette stayed home to take care of the baby and stretch their money until it begged for mercy.

In three years' time, with baby number two on the way, the couple purchased their first house, a "repo-fixer-upper" that measured 1,450 square feet.

They put 15 percent down on the house, and in only nine years their mortgage was paid off. They accomplished all of this on an average annual income of less than $33,000.

Today, the couple feed a family of seven on a monthly grocery budget of $350.

Annette's meal-planning strategy is different from most people's. For one thing, she plans meals for an entire month. And, those meals are based on the best deals she can find at local stores, combined with what she has stored in her pantry and freezer.

Then, the couple select a night (their only grocery shopping trip for the entire month) and spend hours buying the next month's food.

The Economideses also differ from many other couples because they've almost paid off the mortgage on their current house. They have no auto loans or credit card debt, and Annette is a stay-at-home mom who home-schools her children.

The frugal life

Of course, choosing to live without credit had repercussions for the couple. In the early days of their marriage, they were disheartened when a Danish furniture truck pulled up to their apartment complex and delivered beautiful new furniture to their next-door neighbor.

Annette sat on their $25 orange-and-brown-plaid couch, purchased from a missionary, and cried.

Years later, they remained in their cramped, small house while their friends were buying their second or third larger houses.

They wondered if there was something wrong with their plan, but they decided to stay put and to continue paying off their mortgage.

This put them in better shape to buy a new house in 1995, when their previous house became unbearable for them and their five growing children. "We were literally tripping over each other," Steve says.

After months of searching, they moved into a larger house with five bedrooms, one of which they converted to an office/library. As they did with their first house, they began paying extra to reduce their debt.

Putting it in print

Recently, after 20 years of steady employment, Steve and Annette felt the calling to proceed with a dream they had written down more than five years before: *The Home Economiser* newsletter.

On a dog-eared piece of paper in his datebook, Steve has the original outline of what the newsletter would accomplish. The focus and message have been put into a concise statement: "Making the most of your money and your life."

Over the years, the couple dreamed of starting a home business and working on it as a family, but they never felt the Lord's timing until this year.

Now that three of their kids have hit the teen years, a greater need for Steve's presence and involvement in daily family life has provided the impetus for starting the newsletter.

But the current state of the economy, and the many people reeling from major losses of investment/retirement income, also confirm that now is the time!

Why do they skimp and save?

During years of helping families as one-on-one debt counselors and as Crown small group study leaders, the Economideses have seen people hungry for an alternative to the world's way of constant consumption and debt. "The people we've assisted feel hope for the first time in a long time and are more open to hear about God's love and His ability to provide for them," Annette says.

"As Christians, we are called to be salt and light to all people," Steve explains. "Writing and speaking about our tightwad trek has opened the door to share the true source of wealth and peace with thousands of people."

Looking toward the future, the couple say they have big goals, but those goals don't involve worldly toys or pleasures. They just want to live simply, train their five children to be obedient stewards of their resources, and help others dig their way out of debt.

To learn more about Steve and Annette's financial journey, visit their Web site (www.homeeconomiser.com) or send a self-addressed, stamped envelope to HomeEconomiser—Free Sample Issue, PO Box 12603, Scottsdale AZ 85267-2603. Watch for the release of their book, American's Cheapest Family, *by Crown Publishers, a division of Random House, in January, 2007.*

Sign Post

Staying out of debt and living as God calls us to live lead us to function on a different plain from the world. We are salt and light to the world, which impacts the "world" system of constant consumption and debt.

"Then Jesus said to his disciples: "Therefore I tell you, do not worry about your life, what you will eat; or about your body, what you will wear. Life is more than food, and the body more than clothes" (Luke 12:22-23).

Joshua, Tim, Caleb, Leslie, and Anna Alba

Letters to God:

Three kids have a new take on money

WHEN TIM ALBA FINISHED Crown's adult small group study, he wasn't content to just sit on the principles he'd learned. He not only shared those principles with other adults but also with his own children. Tim recognized an important truth: stewardship begins in the home. It's the place where we have the greatest opportunity to influence the next generation—to *"train up a child in the way he should go"* (Proverbs 22:6).

After Tim's church was introduced to Crown, the members began looking at different groups of people, including senior citizens, who would benefit from the study. "I was interested in children," he says. "The time to start training them is when they're young."

When Tim was growing up, his father set a good example for him by being fiscally responsible. But it wasn't until Tim took part in a Crown Bible study that he became fully exposed to everything the Bible says about money. He saw the life-changing power of God's financial principles, and in a society where so many people are looking for happiness, he witnessed one of the most awesome effects of those principles: contentment.

One couple in their 50s told him they wished they had learned the principles 30 years earlier. He and his wife Anna decided to begin a family Bible study based on Crown's materials for teens and children.

They gave their 10-year-old son Caleb a copy of *The Secret*, Crown's study for children. They gave Leslie, age 15, and Joshua, age 13, copies of Crown's teen study, *God's Way of Handling Money*.

When the children completed the studies, Tim asked each of them to write a letter to the Lord, telling Him what they had learned.

Not long after that, during a church dinner, Tim was asked to share some inspirational words. He read the letter that his youngest son Caleb had written, and it received a tremendous response.

"The material taught in the study really grabbed Caleb," Tim says. "For one thing, he realized God had called him to do his best in his homework. Financial principles are not just about being faithful in finances but in all things. And, rather than money being something that keeps us from the Lord, it's something that can draw us to the Lord."

A few weeks into the study, all three children became very involved in the learning process. "It became fun," Tim says. "It was about them and the Lord, not about Dad trying to be cheap. They could have gone into the studies kicking and screaming or with quiet resistance. But it wasn't a stretch for them to participate."

All three of Tim's children are Christians. They study their Bibles, and they are in excellent Sunday school classes.

Still, their dad was surprised to see them giving the same answers to questions as those given by adults in the studies he had led at church. "This helped me to see that God's financial principles are something anyone can grasp," he says.

Caleb says that before learning the principles, he really wasn't sure how to spend the money he received. Like many children, he spent freely, and in a short period of time he would grow tired of the things he had bought.

Tim helps Caleb manage his envelope budgeting system. The Alba children divide their money in to church, ministry, family vacation, and personal spending categories.

Today, all three children are more careful spenders, and they are saving and giving as well. For example, 10 percent of their money goes to the church and five percent goes to ministry. They put 50 percent toward their family vacation, and the other 35 percent goes for whatever they choose.

This is amazing in light of a question Tim answered during a Crown study two years ago. The question was, "What do you want from Crown?" Tim's answer was that he wanted to help children, including his own, develop a biblical perspective on money.

Now, in addition to the change he's seen in Caleb, his daughter Leslie is less affected by all the pressure to buy what everyone else is buying. His older son Joshua realizes that the biblical financial principles his dad emphasizes are from God; they're not just his dad's opinion.

"The beauty of the principles is that once you understand them, they're not hard to remember," says Tim, who's actively involved with Crown in his church and with the ministry's Dallas city team. "The principles become a part of who you are. This is what I wanted for my children. I wanted them to do what was right when no one was watching, and this is especially true for that day when they leave home to go to college and live on their own."

Tim is a corporate controller for Cici's Pizza. He knows the wisdom of handling money wisely, but Crown helped to personalize this wisdom for him, and now it has done the same for his children.

"What has happened in our family is amazing, but it's not because we're anything special," he says. "We're just some average old 'bears' who happen to live in Texas. But when we stand before the Lord, we'll have something worthwhile to give Him because we followed His financial principles. I hope many other families will do the same thing. If they will, it can draw them together in ways they would not have imagined."

Sign Post

 Stewardship begins in the home. Financial principles are not just about being faithful in finances, but in all things. Anyone can grasp the principles. The time to train children is when they are young, when a foundation can be laid. Character is doing what is right when no one is watching.

"We will not hide them from their children; we will tell the next generation the praiseworthy deeds of the Lord, his power, and the wonders he has done" (Psalms 78:4).

Dear Lord:

I thank you for the opportunity you gave us in how to get to spend money wiser and better. I learned that it can make a huge difference when you spend money wiser, and I also learned that by spending money wiser I will have a better life.

When I get older I can get closer to you by money. I learned that you give tithing every month, and all the money in our ministry envelope goes to the Shaws, who need money so they can tell the people about you and other ministries.

All the money in our church envelope will get to the church so they can buy Bibles and things they need to do the lessons to show other people about you. I also learned that when you don't do your chores you don't get money to give to the church and ministries.

In the future I will spend money wiser by using envelopes, and all the chores I do, the money will go to great ministries. So, now I will do my chores to please you and my parents, and I will always tithe 10 percent to the church.

I will also spend money wiser so I can live a better life and not be a lazy bum for the rest of my life, but do what I know is right so I may please you and have a very successful life. Thank you so much God. I will always love you.

Love,
Caleb Alba

Jim and Lisa Hellier, with their sons Matthew, Nate, and Samuel.

Riding the Storm:

Lisa Hellier

By Lisa Hellier

I MARRIED JIM [my husband] right out of college and was more than happy to hand the reins of money management over to him. It was Jim who first introduced me to the principle and privilege of tithing. His father had taught him to tithe at the age of six. The biblical principles Jim learned and applied throughout his childhood, teen, and college years meant we were able to marry without any debt whatsoever and with savings and investment accounts.

A devastating illness

Jim was in the Army our first five and one-half years of marriage. We were living in Fort Leonard Wood, Missouri. I had the radio on all the time, listening to a local Christian radio station and soon began my daily ritual of listening to "Money Matters" from 2:30 p.m. to 3:00 p.m.

Those daily sessions with Steve and Larry were educational, inspiring, and unbeknownst to me, [were] preparing me for future works.

When Jim achieved the rank of Captain, we kept our standard of living at his 1st Lieutenant's pay and put the raise amount into our savings. Our first child [James] was due in 1994 and we felt richly blessed in many ways.

When our son was three and one-half months old he became critically ill, and we embarked on a two-and-a-half-year journey of hospital stays, treatments, and hard decisions.

Just prior to our son's illness, Jim completed the Career Direct® assessment and we planned for his resignation from the service, graduate school, and a career change. All of this transpired in the midst of discovering our son required an immediate bone marrow transplant at Duke University Medical Center in Durham, North Carolina.

I flew ahead with our son while Jim finished his military commitment and traveled to Greenville, South Carolina, to move our belongings into his mom's house. He entered graduate school at Clemson and commuted up to Duke every other weekend to be with us. Our house in Missouri was on the market nine months before it sold. Jim went from making a civilian equivalent of $45,000 a year to making $9,000 a year as a graduate assistant.

Our medical bills were phenomenal, as James required two bone marrow transplants with extensive inpatient stays, chemotherapy, a cord blood transplant, and several intensive care unit stays in addition to travel costs, housing costs, etc.

The strain on us emotionally and physically was greater than the drain on our finances as we were forced to virtually subsist on our savings—savings that we had only because we had instituted biblical financial principles.

James died October 16, 1996, leaving us broken and confused as to why God had allowed this tragedy to happen.

Lisa Hellier

Another wave of trials

The second battering of financial crisis came in the form of creditors for the hundreds of thousands of dollars now owed in medical bills. The largest single bill we ever received was for more than $750,000.

James' care was supposedly covered by [military insurance], but red tape and bureaucracy had left the bills unpaid and the creditors only saw us as defaulters.

Although we had met all of our obligations of deductibles, co-pays, and out-of-pocket expenses, we were hounded in the mail and on the phone for two years after James' death.

Eventually the bulk of the debt was paid by [military insurance] after an attorney friend involved Sen. Strom Thurmond on our behalf. … Jim finished his masters [degree] and we took a job in Macon, Georgia. Once in Georgia, we still had about $450,000 in outstanding medical bills. The greater portion of this was our responsibility and the rest was still due from [military insurance]. Again we involved our then Rep. Saxby Chambliss and the balance was paid. After months of paying $50 a month to pay down the remaining debt, considering bankruptcy, and much prayer, we asked one of our son's former doctors to get involved and ask the hospital to forgive the debt. God intervened mightily and the debt was forgiven.

Launching Crown in Macon

Last year we were contacted by Jerry Howell [with Crown Financial Ministries] and enjoyed a special dinner with him and his wife here in our home.

Jerry encouraged us to consider launching Crown in Macon, but we politely declined, not thinking that the timing was right. So we were pleasantly surprised to have been invited to the Marco Island, Florida "Freedom to Serve" conference this past March.

Every obstacle possible to keep us from attending occurred, but we were dogged in going, hopeful that the training and instruction would give us new breath for our latest venture of starting our own business. The weekend was an incredible blessing and gave us renewed vision and hope for the good works God has ordained for us to do.

Inspired, we came back home and quickly signed up to be trained as [leaders for Crown's small group study]. We are currently in the process of recruiting for our first group.

Please pray that our small group beginnings will impact Macon as a pebble in the pond, that I will be faithful and diligent as I learn to personally manage money as God's steward, and that our business will increase under God's ownership so that we might be able to give more generously to the Kingdom.

Sign Post

 Storms come to all of us. Surviving them and prevailing depend on our being able to hang on to God's Word through them.

"But everyone who hears these words of mine and does not put them into practice is like a foolish man who built his house on sand" (Matthew 7:26).

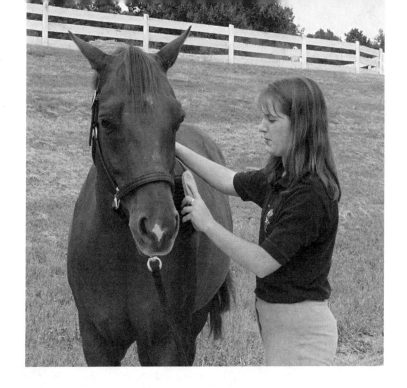

Lord Over All Things:

God Owns It All

By Mindy Cook and Chuck Thompson

ABRAHAM CLIMBED THE MOUNTAIN in the land of Moriah where God had instructed him to sacrifice his son Isaac. To fulfill the Lord's command, he had to recognize that everything he had belonged to God, including his beloved son.

As he climbed higher with Isaac, perhaps he remembered how he and Sarah had struggled to have a child. Perhaps he thought of his son's early years or of God's promise that he

would be the father of a great nation. Genesis 22:11 says that *"the angel of the Lord"* stopped Abraham before he performed the sacrifice. He passed the test, and he went on to become the patriarch of Israel.

Being willing to recognize that God is the real owner of our possessions, including our most cherished things, isn't always easy. But the Bible tells us He owns it all, including *"everything that moves in the field"* (Psalm 50:11).

It's in one of those fields, located near a place called Quillians Corner, in north Georgia, where Captain, a stately, chestnut-colored horse, enjoys running free, basking in the warm sunshine, and sampling the variety of greens growing under his feet. He is the fulfillment of a dream for Mindy Cook, who always wanted a horse of her own. But there was a time when Mindy had to acknowledge who Captain's real owner was.

That acknowledgment was part of a process that began in the spring of 2002. During the week of May 5, Mindy was involved with two productions being presented by her drama class at Heritage Academy in Gainesville, Georgia.

"God had been working in my life the whole spring, and He was beginning to teach me how great and unchanging He is," she says. "During the week of May 5th, I received a crash course in the stability of God."

On Tuesday of that week, she learned that a friend, Myra Satterfield, who had coached her in two separate sports, had been killed in a car accident. "I really admired and loved [Myra]," Mindy says. "Her death made me start thinking about my own mortality and about the mortality of the people and things I loved. I also started questioning God. 'Why did you let this happen?' It seemed so senseless. But He gently assured me that He was in control."

A time of decision

Earlier in the spring, Mindy's dad, John Cook, a local banker, told her he wanted her to have her own checking account. But as a prerequisite, she had to complete Crown's teen study, *God's Way of Handling Money*. She agreed.

"I had no clue what an impact the study would have on my life," Mindy says. "I found that I actually enjoyed it. It was very informative, and it took me deep into God's Word."

Mindy was working on the study during the week of May 5th. And on Thursday of that week, she was learning about Christians' responsibility as stewards and God's ownership of all things.

"Part of the study workbook was a Quit Claim Deed, which was designed for me to sign over all my possessions to God," she says. "As I thought about what to put on the deed, God helped me look deep inside myself. I looked around my room and thought about everything I saw, and I asked myself, 'How would I feel if it were destroyed.' "

Among the items Mindy considered were her pictures and model horses, which had a lot of sentimental value. However, she could do without them. Then, she considered her most treasured possessions: her animals. How would she feel if they were taken away?

"I didn't even want to think about it, but God did," she says. "The question wouldn't go away. Could I give Captain, my horse, to God? I had owned him for over two years and was pretty possessive about him. I had wanted a horse for my whole life, and now that I finally had one, I certainly did not want to give him up. But God kept pressing, 'Give him to me. I made him. Don't you think I know what's best for him and for you?' "

At that point, Mindy listed Captain as the first possession on her Quit Claim Deed. She felt as though a burden had been lifted from her heart. And, it made writing the next item on the list, "Spencer the dog," a little easier.

"The possessions that followed seemed trivial compared to these two," she says. "I concluded the list with, 'Any other possessions not mentioned.' "

The storm

That evening, Mindy's dad arrived early at drama rehearsal to pick her up. When she sat down in the car, he asked to hold her hand. His actions, and the tone of his voice, brought back memories of the day her mom informed her about Coach Sattefield's death. What else was wrong? The first thing Mindy's dad told her was that her horse was okay. But something had happened earlier that day at Avalon Hills Equestrian Center, where Captain is boarded.

"There had been a big storm at the barn," Mindy says. "Lightning struck a tree in the pasture, where Captain and his herd were grazing. The lightning traveled through the ground toward the barn manager's metal trailer.

"Captain and his buddy, Apache, were standing behind the trailer, and the lightning struck both of them. The force of the lightning threw both of them to the ground. Apache was killed instantly."

The aftermath

Although Captain was knocked down, he was able to get up. Then, he and the other horses stood guard around Apache.

A veterinarian examined Captain and was amazed that he was still alive. But even more surprising was the fact that he had no burns—not even singed tail hairs.

The vet said to Mindy's mom, Beth Cook, "Tell your little girl to thank Jesus."

Never before had he seen two horses be struck by lightning and one of them survive. Outside of some swelling in his legs as a result of his fall, Captain had no injuries at all.

"Every time I see Captain, I am reminded that God is the only One we can lean on," Mindy says. "He is the only constant in life. People and things may come and go, but God is there forever.

"A few weeks ago, the second possession on my deed, Spencer the dog, died. I miss him terribly, but he is God's and God knows what is best, for him and for me.

"Through the Crown study, God helped me let go of my earthly possessions. He has shown me I can't rely on them to be there. I am very grateful that He lets me ride His horse, Captain."

Sign Post

 In spite of how we feel, it's important to know that God owns everything we love and cherish.

" … *for every animal of the forest is mine, and the cattle on a thousand hills" (Psalms 50:10).*

LHDs are the second-largest class of ships in the U.S. Navy, behind aircraft carriers. It was on one of these ships, the USS Kearsarge, that Mary led the Crown study during a six-month deployment.

On Land or on Sea:

Taking Crown Around the World

GOD'S WISDOM IS FOR EVERYONE, regardless of their circumstances, who they are, or the country in which they live. Thus, Christians should be ready to share that wisdom both "in season and out of season" no matter where they find themselves (2 Timothy 4:2).

Mary Graves, a Medical Service Corps officer with the U.S. Navy, lives by this principle. She defines Crown as the "love of her life," and she literally has shared it on land and on sea.

The daughter of a pastor, Mary was led to the Lord by her father when she was 5 years old. She was born in Los Angeles and has lived in many places, but she counts Mississippi as her home. It was there that she received her bachelor's degree at Jackson State University.

Afterward, she attended the Washington University School of Medicine in Saint Louis, where she majored in health administration and human resources management. She completed her education through a scholarship program offered by the U.S. Navy.

A financial fast

While working on her graduate degree in Saint Louis, Mary attended a group sponsored by Bible Study Fellowship International. And, she was reading a chapter a day from *The Complete Guide to Managing Your Money* by Larry Burkett.

Inspired by the financial principles Larry shared, she began a 30-day "financial fast" in which she kept a close watch on her spending.

She also kept a prayer journal and followed the principles of a popular acronym based on the word "pray":

P—praise God,

R—repent,

A—ask on behalf of others, and

Y—ask on behalf of yourself last.

She shared what she was doing with her Bible study group, and one of them recommended that she take Crown's small group study.

But within two weeks, Mary was caught up in the process of graduating from Washington University and moving to Detroit.

After she arrived there, the first church she attended was the same church where Brian and Chris Gettel, Crown trainers and coordinators in Detroit, were members. Inside the church program was information about Crown.

Mary felt God was confirming the advice she had received back in Saint Louis, and she signed up for a fall 1997 Crown class led by Jess and Carol Livermore.

"I saw my leaders model faithfulness and love for God and their students," she says. "I loved the class so much that I wanted to find out what else I could do. That's when I asked about training to be one of the Crown leaders."

Crown in Japan

Mary was in Detroit only one year. However, she was able to lead a Crown class before she went on assignment with the Navy in Okinawa, Japan, where personnel from various branches of the military are stationed.

She talked to the Navy chaplain in Okinawa about starting Crown there. He agreed, and she led a small group of six people.

"One year later, we had 26 graduates, eight newly-trained leaders, and 30 students on the waiting list," Mary says.

As a result of the class, she saw marriages strengthened. And, one woman decided to start a class for teen children of military personnel using Crown's teen study, *God's Way of Handling Money.*

"I was there only 20 months, so it was hard to get everything started and then train somebody to stay there, but Crown is still going in Okinawa," Mary says.

Crown at sea

After leaving Japan, Mary was stationed aboard the USS Kearsarge, a Landing Helicopter Deck (LHD) ship, which had some 3,500 Navy and Marine personnel aboard.

The LHDs are second in size to the aircraft carriers, the largest ships in the Navy's fleet.

Mary was assigned to the USS Kearsarge for six months, and she approached the ship's chaplain about having a Crown group on board the ship.

She also contacted Mark Murray, a volunteer with Crown's international outreach, who provided her with the logistical support she needed to implement Crown on board the ship.

Ten people signed up for the class, and what was supposed to be a 12-week study stretched out over the entire six-month deployment due to all the interruptions and conflicting schedules on board a Navy vessel.

"Our workday was normally from 6 a.m. to about 5 p.m. or 6 p.m. in the evening," Mary says. "But emergencies and unexpected issues would often prevent all of us from getting together."

Some of the emergencies that occurred during this time included the following.

• A military aircraft crashed into the ocean near the Kearsarge, and the five crew members had to be rescued.

• A young man on another ship was decapitated in a tragic accident.

• A woman with a tubal pregnancy required emergency surgery. She survived and recovered.

"Our whole environment was constantly changing," Mary says. But despite all the challenges around her and other members of the Crown group, Mary says they "witnessed people paying off debt and renewing their fellowship with God—all through the power of prayer and applying His Word."

One man had been estranged from his father, and just before his father passed away, he was able to forgive him and tell him he was sorry.

Mary says the Crown group was a "family away from family" that provided love, support, and encouragement to its members. One occasion when that "family" was needed most was September 2001. The USS Kearsarge was just leaving Turkey when people on board the ship learned about the 9/11 attacks. In response, members of the Crown group knelt and prayed together.

Three of the students graduated and completed all 12 lessons. The rest had early transfers, emergency leave, and/or changes in job assignments and schedules.

Still sharing the message

Today, Mary serves as comptroller at the Naval Dental Center in Norfolk, Virginia. She lives in Virginia Beach and attends Azalea Garden Church, which is holding its first Crown class in January 2004.

In addition, she is serving on Crown's Tidewater-Virginia Beach City Team, led by Randy and Kelly Cadwallader.

"When God gives you a gift, you have a strong desire to share it immediately with everyone," Mary says. "You can't keep it to yourself, because it is so powerful. For me, Crown has been a gift from God. It's a gift I am blessed to share with people everywhere and anywhere, whether in the U.S., Japan, or on board a Navy vessel."

Sign Post

 Regardless of your circumstances, God's wisdom is for you. As a Christian, you should be willing to share this wisdom with people wherever you are.

"And the things you have heard me say in the presence of many witnesses entrust to reliable men who will also be qualified to teach others" (2 Timothy 2:2).

Allen, Mitchell, and Debbie Lovins. The drawing in the background features all three of the couple's boys and was done by an artist who combined portions of various family photos.

Trust in the Midst of Trials:

Allen and Debbie Lovins

SOMETIMES THE ROUTINE, MINOR EVENTS of our lives prepare us for major crises that we did not expect. At such times we look back and realize God was strengthening us for what lay ahead.

Allen and Debbie Lovins have experienced this preparation in their own lives. It happened at Arbor Heights Baptist Church, in Douglasville, Georgia, where their pastor, Andy Gray, introduced them to Crown's small group study.

"Debbie and I were saved later in life," Allen says. "We were in our 30s and really knew nothing about God's plan for managing money. We had sought the American dream, trying to have the things we wanted, and we tried to finance most of that as we went. But we didn't get very far."

After accepting Christ as their Savior, the couple wanted to please God and properly manage the resources He had entrusted to them. In January of 1997, when they were given the opportunity to participate in the small group study, they accepted.

A lot more than money

"One of the greatest aspects of the study was learning how far-ranging stewardship actually is," Allen says. "In one of the first classes we had a Quit Claim Deed on which we symbolically surrendered our possessions back to God. We acknowledged that all that we possessed did, in fact, belong to Him."

As Allen prepared for the class, he realized he couldn't list everything he owned on the deed. So, he considered the things most dear to him—the things that might come between God and himself. The first thing he listed was his family.

Allen and Debbie had three sons: Adam, who was almost 17; Daniel, age 14; and Mitchell, age 10. The three boys loved outdoor activities with their dad, including fishing, camping, and hunting. They also enjoyed soccer and other sports.

In addition, they were heavily involved with the youth group at Arbor Heights, and on Saturday, May 10, 1997, Adam and Daniel went with some friends from church to play tennis in the morning.

When they were done, Adam drove home with his brother Daniel in the passenger seat. He lost control of his car in a curve and it veered off the road and struck a tree. Daniel was dead at the scene, and Adam was taken to a local hospital. A series of tests determined that he was brain dead, and Allen and Debbie had to make the difficult decision to remove his body from life support.

Firmly committed

"I had to look back at what I had told God," Allen says. "I had given Him my children. I had acknowledged that they were His and that He had just given me care over them. I really had to do some soul-searching. I understood that I really did mean what I said and that I had to surrender to God's will in that aspect of our lives.

"It was not easy to give them up. It was a traumatic experience. We still suffer daily with it, even though it's been six years. But I do know that God is in control and that His plan is perfect, even when I don't understand it.

"I don't know what we would have done had we not been through that study. I'm sure that, somehow, God would have gotten us through it. But I am convinced, with all of my heart, that the study was the primary tool He used to prepare us for the road that He had chosen to take us down."

A wish fulfilled

Prior to Adam's death, he and his dad had watched a television program about a young man who had received a heart transplant. At that time, Adam told his dad that if anything ever happened to him, he wanted his organs to be used to help someone else.

Allen and Debbie honored his wish, and his heart was given to a young man in Dallas, Georgia who was about Adam's age. Today, at age 23, that young man is a minister, and he is conducting revivals with his dad. Adam's corneas, kidneys, and liver also benefited other people who needed organ donations.

"It has been a tremendous joy to know that through our tragedy and through our heartache, someone else has been able to gain joy and experience pleasure," Allen says. "It's also good to know that through this young man's preaching, lives are being impacted and souls are being saved for God's Kingdom—for eternity."

Looking back on her and Allen's experience, Debbie says one of the biggest adjustments she had to make during the Crown study was recognizing that stewardship went far beyond money.

"I learned that everything belonged to God," she says. "One of the hardest things for me to accept was that my children were His, but it really helped me prepare for what lay ahead. I was really glad that God put us in that class ahead of time to prepare us."

Bringing hope to others

Another adjustment for Allen was his career. He had gone through a couple of studies on spiritual gifts and had learned that his primary gift is exhortation.

"I had the hardest time trying to figure out how an encourager is supposed to function in the church," he says. "One of the things I learned is that God takes someone who has the gift of exhortation and uses their life experiences. He takes the highs and the lows and uses them to mold that person into someone who can relate to others regardless of where they're at in their lives."

Today, through his career, Allen has the perfect environment in which to exercise his spiritual gift. Following the accident, he quit his job of 23 years, wondering how he could learn to do anything else. But he realized that, if God could get him through the loss of his boys, He could also get him through a career change.

Allen and Debbie purchased a small home furnishings business in Villa Rica, Georgia, and afterward, God began to bring people in need to their doorstep. "One of the things I see God doing on a regular basis is to bring people into our store who need encouragement more than they need retail goods," Allen says. "We meet total strangers who are willing to pour their hearts out and say, 'You know, I'm hurting today.' And God has equipped us to say, 'You know, I've been there, and it'll be okay, because God is in control.' "

Sign Post

 Stewardship includes being responsible for all that God has given you—the things with which He has blessed you and the loved ones in your life. All belong to the Lord, and we have the privilege of being His stewards.

"May the God of peace, who through the blood of the eternal covenant brought back from the dead our Lord Jesus, that great Shepherd of the sheep, equip you with everything good for doing his will, and may he work in us what is pleasing to him, through Jesus Christ, to whom be glory for ever and ever. Amen" (Hebrews 13:20-21).

Nelson (front row, right) with some of the men he has assisted through his work with U-Turn for Christ's ranch discipleship program in Greeneville, Tennessee.

Off the Streets:

Nelson Morais Found a Heavenly Home

NELSON MORAIS' GOAL IN LIFE was to be a journalist, and he got off to a good start by earning a journalism degree from the University of Southern California.

After graduation he managed to find some newspaper work, but not enough to support himself. He took jobs in word processing and sales, and eventually wound up in a sales position in San Diego.

"It really wasn't paying very much," he says. "I was frustrated with it, but I think one of the reasons I was frustrated is that a lot of people in the company were Christians, and I wasn't."

In 1992, Nelson packed some belongings into his car and headed east with $400 in his pocket. He hoped to find a job as a journalist, get settled, and have his sister ship him the rest of his belongings. It never happened.

He ran out of money in West Palm Beach, Florida. Unable to buy gasoline for his car, he parked it at a convenience store. The clerk on duty at the time gave him permission to leave his car at the store, but the next clerk wasn't aware of the arrangement and had his car towed.

Suddenly homeless

"I thought I'd find a job and maybe, in a couple of weeks, I'd be able to pay the fine and get my car back," Nelson says. "It didn't work out, and I became homeless. It was a real shock to me, but as time passed by, I began to think God was wanting me to be homeless. It was only after I was saved a couple of years ago that I realized it was Satan telling me this, not God."

Satan had gained a foothold in Nelson's life through the influence of a psychic, whom Nelson had been paying to advise him. The psychic claimed to represent God, but she led Nelson to practice rituals like burning candles at certain times of day and avoiding certain types of people.

Nelson is pictured at U-Turn's headquarters in California. In the background is a pig, the "honored guest" at the ministry's annual pig roast

For the next five and one-half years, he drifted between Florida and North Carolina, hitchhiking from one place to another. "Several times I was caught on minor charges because, being homeless, you kind of stick out like a sore thumb," he says.

But after a while, Nelson saw benefits in going to jail from time to time because it gave him three meals and a warm place to sleep. Otherwise, he was sleeping in abandoned buildings, in cardboard boxes, and on construction sites, using his shoes as a pillow. Sometimes he slept in homeless shelters, where he heard the Gospel preached.

He took a variety of short-term jobs but knew nothing about handling money. So, if he swept floors on a construction site and earned $30 for one day, he would simply go out and blow the money that night. Unable to retain money, he began taking jobs like picking up trash at fast food restaurants in exchange for a meal.

Getting arrested, again

One day, when Nelson was in Georgia, he grew tired of being on the streets. Hoping to be arrested and spend a couple of weeks in jail, he sat down in someone's car. When the car's owner returned, Nelson refused to talk with him. Likewise, he refused to talk with the police when they arrived.

He did end up in jail, but this time he was facing a felony charge and up to five years behind bars.

"That kind of jolted me," he says. "I tried on my own to get a court appearance and get out of jail sooner, but that didn't happen. So, I finally wrote to my cousin, whose address I could remember. This was my first contact with any family members for about six years."

Nelson's sister came to his aid, and with her help, he was released from jail. She took him back to California, and he lived with her for a while.

He took some word processing courses, worked as a temporary legal secretary, and eventually moved out of his sister's house and found a place to live. But just as he was getting back on his feet, he felt he was being called to return to the streets. He went back East and took up the homeless lifestyle again.

A change of heart

In 1999, Nelson was in Johnson City, Tennessee, going to restaurants and asking for food, when someone saw him and provided him a temporary place to live. Nelson began attending Calvary Chapel in Greeneville, Tennessee, and through the influence and witness of his pastor, Gary Hall, he accepted Christ as his Savior.

Gary and his wife Isabel took Nelson into their home for a couple of months, and Isabel taught him to budget using Crown's *Family Financial Workbook*.

Nelson found a job at a Taco Bell in Greeneville and got his own apartment. He has since found a higher-paying job as a waiter at a Ryan's restaurant in Greeneville, and in a recent month, his income was 50 percent higher than he had projected. In addition, he has been able to put his journalism skills to use by helping to write a book about a woman in a local nursing home who had been a pioneer in the civil rights movement.

Today, Nelson is thankful that, although he drank some alcohol and took some drugs during the years he was homeless, he never reached the point of addiction.

"I thank God for that," he says. "I could have easily fallen into that if I had gone just a little bit further."

However, he has not forgotten those whose lives have been wrecked by substance abuse. He now works with U-Turn for Christ, a nationwide discipleship ranch program that helps individuals overcome alcohol and drug abuse.

U-Turn uses a multi-phase program, and when individuals at the Greeneville ranch graduate to the second phase, Nelson is there to help them learn budgeting.

"My life has changed," he says. "I try to get into God's Word in the morning and spend time in prayer. I try to work with U-Turn about two days per week. I'm also editing a newsletter that the ministry publishes.

"I'm glad I can pass the budgeting information along to the guys in the U-Turn program. Being on a budget has been a blessing. A lot of people think it's restrictive. Yes, there are certain things that are restrictive, but it also gives you freedom and it gives you peace of mind. I think that's very important."

Sign Post

Having a budget is responsible. Budgeting might seem restrictive at times, but ultimately it brings freedom and peace of mind as we practice stewardship of God's money.

"But the one who received the seed that fell on good soil is the man who hears the word and understands it. He produces a crop, yielding a hundred, sixty or thirty times what was sown" (Matthew 13:23).

God and Our Work:

Justin Barnes

MANY YOUNG PEOPLE WOULD ENVY JUSTIN BARNES. He had a great academic role model—his mom was valedictorian of her class. While he was in college, he was able to work, and get paid, in the career for which he was preparing. Unlike many of his peers, he wasn't burdened by student loan debt. And, after graduating from the University of Georgia with a high GPA, he landed a job that could be paying him a six-figure salary next year.

Now, he's giving it up to serve as an intern at Crossroads Community Church near Lawrenceville, Georgia. The job will require him to raise his own support.

Then and now

"In college, all I talked about was the money I was going to make when I got out," Justin says. "That was my main focus."

He graduated debt free with a double major in finance and management information systems. He paid for his education by working three years as a salaried intern at the help desk in the computer center of UGA's College of Business.

Justin (left) is one of four people doing an internship at Crossroads. He is pictured with Cory Lebovitz, who'll be working with college students.

The job came as the result of what he calls a "random e-mail," in which he inquired about job openings at the computer center.

With an in-demand major and a GPA of more than 3.5, Justin was able to be selective with the job offers he received.

He graduated in May 2003, and the following month he took a job as an information technology (IT) broker—a sales position that would allow him to make $125,000 to $150,000 in the second year.

Justin was well on his way to achieving that goal. After a long training period, he sold more than his quota in the first two months of work.

His job involves buying and selling pre-owned IT hardware, and he deals with people all over the world. During the first half of the day, he's on the phone with people in places like Britain, Scotland, and South Africa. In the afternoon he's talking to people in the U.S.

"When I was in school, this was the type of position I wanted," Justin says. "But the last couple of months, the

Lord's really laid it down that this isn't where He wants me to be."

A Crown graduate, Justin believes the homework involved with the ministry's small group study helped draw him closer to God.

Some of the lessons his dad taught him were like those found in the study, including the warnings about debt.

But Justin says one of the lessons in the study that affected him most is God's ownership of all things. "It's really helping me with this internship idea," he says. "It's not my money anyway. It's God's money."

Thanks to his dad, who served as a deacon, and his mother, a Sunday school teacher, Justin grew up with a biblical foundation.

As a college senior, he developed a strong interest in Bible study, which paved the way for his entry into Crown. He says he was interested to learn that someone had actually developed a study on the financial teachings of God's Word.

A desire to help kids
Before he made his decision to become an intern, Justin felt himself being drawn toward ministry. As he sought the path he needed to follow, he considered overseas work. But when he learned about the internship at Crossroads, he knew that was where he belonged.

In June, he begins two years of service with the church. He'll be one of four interns who'll be working in different sections of Crossroads' ministry.

"My section is going to be middle school students," he says. "There are so many kids who need help, and there's just not enough workers. If I don't take this on full time, I'm cheating the students. I'm not giving it my all, as God required.

"I've tried to do it part time, and God keeps letting me know that He wants me to be full time. It'll be mostly kids here in the church. We have about 175 on Sunday mornings and more than 100 on Wednesday nights."

Justin's duties as an intern will include speaking to large groups of young people, preparing lessons, and serving as a small group leader. "In the small groups, you get to know the kids a lot," he says. "We also make sure they understand the lessons they hear in the big groups and see how those lessons relate to their lives."

When asked if he's considering seminary, Justin says, "I don't see myself in seminary right now, but I didn't see myself taking this position a year ago, either. Right now, I'm thinking more of doing overseas missions after this, maybe somewhere like Africa or Australia.

"I'm starting to listen to God. I heard Him before, but I just wasn't listening. He was leading me toward ministry back in the summer."

Regarding the group to which he'll be assigned, Justin says he has a strong desire to work with middle school kids. "They're at an impressionable age," he adds. "They're doing things I never thought of when I was in middle school.

"I like this age group. I think it's overlooked a lot of times because it's a challenge, but this is the time when kids can begin turning one way or the other. Many kids fall at this age and take a downward spiral. I want to be a good influence on them, because many of them don't have fathers. They need a godly role model."

Sign Post

 Doing God's will won't work on a part-time basis, either in stewardship or things He has revealed to you to do.

"You are the salt of the earth. But if the salt loses its saltiness, how can it be made salty again? It is no longer good for anything, except to be thrown out and trampled by men" *(Matthew 5:13).*

Lloyd Copenbarger counsels a young couple.

It's God's Business:

The "Ministry" of Lloyd Copenbarger

NOT EVERY CHRISTIAN can be the pastor of a church, the founder of a ministry, or the leader of a great evangelistic organization. In fact, many Christians labor each week in the secular workplace. But just because they aren't in "ministry" doesn't mean they can't impact the world for Christ.

During the past 20 years, Lloyd Copenbarger has used his law practice to impact God's Kingdom in a big way. His efforts have resulted in hundreds of millions of dollars being set aside to further the Gospel throughout the world.

More than a job

Lloyd sees his entry into the legal field as more than a general career decision. In his mind, it was a calling. "I got involved in law school because two professors, unbeknownst to each other, told me I should consider becoming an attorney," he says. "I remembered the Scripture that says, 'In the mouth of two or three witnesses shall every word be established.' And I thought, if two people see those qualities in me, I'd better pay attention."

After earning his undergraduate and law degrees from the University of Oklahoma, Lloyd entered the workplace.

He went on to serve as counsel to Dr. Bill Bright, founder of Campus Crusade for Christ, in the late 1970s and early 1980s.

At the time, Dr. Bright was involved in a fund-raising campaign called "Here's Life," which encouraged Christians to give a billion dollars to God's Kingdom by the year 2000 in hopes of funding the Great Commission.

Lloyd was appointed to head Campus Crusade's Great Commission Foundation.

One focus of the Here's Life campaign was wealthy donors who could make substantial gifts.

But Dr. Bright didn't want to overlook people in other income groups, who provided the main support for his organization.

To meet their needs, Lloyd helped to develop seminars that taught people how to use wills and trusts to continue their giving even after death.

The seminars were held primarily in churches closely affiliated with Campus Crusade.

Keeping a good idea alive

When Lloyd left Campus Crusade, the seminar program ceased to operate within the organization.

But people in the churches where he had presented the seminars asked him to continue the program. He agreed.

"The first church we worked with was a church of probably 600 members," Lloyd says, "and there was almost $4 million in gifts to that church, to its mission program, and to organizations like Campus Crusade, Focus on the Family, and other ministries that I felt were God-ordained ministries."

After presenting the seminar in other churches, Lloyd was astounded at the results.

"I had been very much impressed by the billion-dollar campaign and the goals that Dr. Bright had established," he says. "So, I made a private vow. I pledged to the Lord that if He would give me the health and the strength and the opportunity, we would do seminars in churches any place we were given an opportunity—regardless of size, regardless of economic situation—until we had helped God's people make gifts of a billion dollars to the Kingdom through wills and trusts."

Lloyd speaks at the dedication of the Eugene and Billie Yeager Center at California Baptist University.

Lloyd believes his organization reached its $1 billion goal about a year ago.

Afterward, he met with his son and other members of his law firm, Lloyd Copenbarger and Associates, headquartered in Newport Beach, California.

They determined to press on with Lloyd's original vision, and they set the goal of helping Christians give another $1 billion to God's Kingdom.

The seminars presented by Lloyd's firm include a video presentation that contains the basic information people need to ensure the security of their estates, to provide for their loved ones, and to give to the causes that are important to them.

Although Lloyd doesn't solicit gifts to churches and ministries, he encourages people to consider making these gifts through their wills and trusts.

As a result, they can continue their giving legacy, to the organizations of their choice, after they've gone home to be with the Lord.

But as successful as Lloyd has been, there's a lot more to be done. Based on information from his estate planning work, he estimates that 70 percent or more of Christians have no will or trust. This is tragic for all families involved, but it's especially tragic in cases involving young children. If both parents die, the children could end up in the care of a state-appointed guardian who does not share the parents' religious beliefs.

A long association with Crown

One element of Crown's small group study is that participants are encouraged to make a will.

Lloyd saw the results of this while working with a Bakersfield, California church that heavily promoted the Crown program. The church invited Lloyd to speak year after year, and during this time, he was able to observe the impact of the small group study on the congregation.

"We noticed a significant difference in the preparation and giving motivation of the people who had gone through Crown," he says. "Then, several years ago, the Church on the Way, Jack Hayford's church, asked us to come and do an estate planning seminar at the conclusion of their Crown programs. The results were off the chart. I had never dealt with a situation that was as productive, both from the standpoint of people being prepared and motivated to provide protection for their families and to provide for the Kingdom."

Lloyd and his wife Laura are shown at the dedication with CBU President Dr. Ronald L Ellis. The theme for the fund-raising campaign was Opening Doors to the Future.

Lloyd became acquainted with Jim Sullivan, who now serves as Crown's Western area director.

Later, he had an opportunity to meet with Crown cofounders Howard Dayton and Larry Burkett—only a few months before Larry went home to be with the Lord.

For Lloyd, this was the second facet of a long association with Crown. During his time with Campus Crusade, he had become acquainted with Larry, who worked for Dr. Bright in the 1970s.

"I've been involved as a local booster and a financial booster of Crown," Lloyd says. "I feel that is one of the more productive things I can do to support the Kingdom."

Looking back on what God has already accomplished through his firm, Lloyd says he can't take any credit for what's been done.

"It was the Lord who gave me the vision," he says, noting that unforeseen events, orchestrated by God, were what made the achievement of the $1 billion goal possible. "This is the

Lord's ministry. I've just been privileged to have a little part in helping God's people."

Sign Post

 Part of being a good steward is providing for your family after your death. It is estimated that only about thirty percent of Christians have prepared a will or trust to help their families after their death.

"A good man leaves an inheritance for his children's children, but a sinner's wealth is stored up for the righteous" (Proverbs 13:22).

No Longer a Skeptic:

Ken Atkins' Company Honors God

KEN ATKINS is a sixth generation Floridian. His dad was a successful dentist, and his grandfather, a mechanical engineer, was among three scientists who patented the process for making frozen orange juice concentrate.

Growing up in Winter Haven, Florida, Ken was blessed—from a material standpoint. His family had a nice home, new cars, properties, and horses.

They celebrated Thanksgiving and Christmas and prayed before meals, but Ken wasn't brought up in church.

In fact, he learned to be wary of churches, believing that they were places where fanatics and hypocrites congregated.

A career, a house, a lot of debt

Following in his grandfather's footsteps, Ken decided to become an engineer. He earned an ROTC scholarship that paid for his first four years of higher education.

As a senior, he was called out of college to attend officer training school during Operation Desert Storm. But after Iraq quickly succumbed to the U.S. and other allied forces, his officer training class was the first that didn't have to go to the Middle East.

He entered the Army Reserves in 1990 and went on to earn a master's degree in engineering. He left active Reserve duty in 2003.

"After Desert Storm, I started to work as a civil engineer in Orlando," says Ken, who married his wife, Maria, at age 20.

He remembers Larry Burkett saying that some young couples look at their parents' possessions and forget that those possessions were accumulated over many years.

These couples try to match what their parents own in less than five years, which results in tremendous debt.

"I tried to obtain everything my family had, and it caused a lot of problems," Ken says. "Maria and I both had new cars, we bought a house, and we bought everything to furnish the house. We lived in downtown Orlando in an old home, and when we moved in, everything broke." Almost overnight, the couple had accumulated a mortgage, family loans, and $55,000 in additional debt.

Far away from God

In addition, Maria, who had grown up in church, stopped attending church after she met Ken.

"I led her away rather than her leading me toward Christ," he says. "I didn't want anything to do with the church. I felt that it was bondage and that it was people telling me how to run my life, which is what I had been taught."

Ken was hired by a university to teach engineering in the evenings, and during his drive to work, he began listening to J. Vernon McGee's "Through the Bible" radio program.

Ken's family experienced a miracle when his wife Maria gave birth to a boy, whom they named Isaac. Their three adopted children are excited about the addition of a new member to the family. Pictured (left to right) are Ken, Isaac, Maria, Lilee, Noah, and Eli.

"He happened to be talking about Vietnam vets, which kind of interested me, being a lieutenant in the Reserves at the time," Ken says. "Then, I came across Larry Burkett and his program. I really didn't care for the Christian content, but I knew Larry had worked with NASA, and that interested me. He was down to earth and completely different from some of the showy televangelists I had seen while flipping through channels on the television."

During this time, Ken was carrying about 12 credit cards and shifting the balance from one card to another in order to stay ahead. But his debt grew harder and harder to manage.

About one year later, Ken's platoon went on a two-week training exercise. As a lieutenant, he was in the command center, where he had access to a radio that allowed him to hear 14 straight days of Larry Burkett broadcasts. At the end of that time, he accepted Christ as his Savior.

A financial wake-up call

While he was in the field, Ken contracted an illness that he believes was malaria. He suffered from a 103-degree fever for several days, and during this time, he dreamed that he died.

He could see his wife struggling with the financial problems he had left behind.

When his fever finally broke, and he was able to get back on his feet, he began taking action to change his financial situation.

He and Maria began tithing, attending First Baptist in Orlando, and growing in their faith. "I read everything there was to read that Larry had ever published and just became a real fan of his ministry and began to support it," Ken says.

Based on advice he received from the ministry, Ken contacted Consumer Credit Counseling Service and began paying off his debt.

"In four years we paid off all the $55,000 we owed," he says. "I was making a base engineer's salary, which was not enough to pay off the debt in four years. But God blessed us in enormous ways. We got income tax refunds we weren't expecting, checks from title companies and insurance companies, and dividend checks."

Growing in knowledge

Like many people who've benefited from God's financial principles, Ken wanted to help others. He completed Crown's budget counselor training course, and just last year he completed the ministry's small group study.

After reading the testimony of Ken Gossage in the second issue of *Dividends*, he also went through the ministry's *Career Direct*® assessment with his business partner, Jonathon Bray.

Blessings at work and at home

Based on principles from Larry Burkett's *Business by the Book*, Ken and Jonathon started their own engineering company.

Another miracle for Ken is the success of his engineering business, which he started with fellow Christian Jonathan Bray (pictured here).

Other people told them that their company would not succeed if they kept their commitment to:

• give 10 percent of their gross business income to the Lord's work and

• close at least half a day on Thursdays in order to volunteer for Crown.

At first, the company had a single client who built one home per year. Within a couple of months, it had about 15 clients, and within one year it was debt free.

Last year the company grossed $300,000, and Ken and Jonathon were able to give $30,000 to God's work.

However, Ken's blessings have gone far beyond the financial realm. During his and Maria's 15-year marriage, they had been unable to have children. They adopted three children ages 6, 5, and 4.

"We were not supposed to be able to have children," Ken says. "They told us there was no chance, but my wife just delivered a baby. And, our other three children are glad to have another sibling.

"Without Crown, I know I wouldn't be where I am today. I read Crown materials in my spare time, and I think I've just about read everything the ministry has produced. Jonathon and I even have a Crown library in our office. So, without doubt, Larry Burkett and Howard Dayton's ministry has really changed my life, and it continues to do so."

Ken is doing double duty as he manages his engineering business and takes care of his son Isaac.

Sign Post

Ken honored God in his business in two ways: by tithing income to the Lord's work, and by setting aside specific hours in the business week to minister to others. From being heavily in debt to operating a prosperous business, Crown has helped bring life to Ken's family.

"Jesus replied, 'What is impossible with men is possible with God'" (Luke 18:27).

Faithful Witnesses:
Mike and Liz Simpson

IN 1986, MIKE AND LIZ SIMPSON were introduced to Larry Burkett's *How to Manage Your Money* Bible study. After completing the material, they followed up by establishing a budget using Larry's *Family Financial Workbook.*

"It changed our whole thinking," Mike says, "especially as far as tithing was concerned." One key lesson the couple learned was tithing from their first fruits (Proverbs 3:9).

At the time, they were living in California. Their church didn't put a lot of emphasis on biblical financial teaching, and their pastor mentioned money from the pulpit only about once a year.

Mike didn't want to become caught up in legalistic thinking about money because he was "under grace." He laughs about it now, noting it was just an excuse to avoid tithing.

The study also prompted the couple to deal with another key issue: debt. "We had some small debts like credit cards, and another small loan, that we cleared up quickly," Mike says. "Then, we started working on our house. Within three and one-half years we were totally debt free and have been ever since."

A personal ministry

After their lives were changed by the Bible study and financial workbook, the Simpsons began sharing these materials with others through Bible studies in their home and church.

When they moved to Bend, Oregon seven years ago, they continued this ministry, and they're now in the midst of another study with three couples.

"It hasn't been anything that we've pushed," Mike says. "Sometimes there would be nine or 10 months in which we wouldn't do a study. On other occasions they'd be back-to-back.

"It looks like that's going to be the situation in the near future, because people's lives are changed, the word gets out, they tell other people, and here we go again. There are a lot of hurting people out there, and we're thrilled to see what the Lord is doing."

Mike and Liz attend Oasis Christian Fellowship, a growing body of believers that was brought together by a local pastor who originally intended to plant a church in another state, possibly as far away as New York.

He now shepherds a group of people who previously were not connected to any particular fellowship in the area. The group currently meets in a home, and on a recent Sunday, 50 people were present.

In order to accommodate their fellowship's growth, Mike, Liz, and the other people at Oasis are looking to rent a larger meeting place. And, as this growth continues, the couple will be there to share God's financial principles with the members who will form the foundation of the church.

Changed lives

Among the people Mike and Liz have taught throughout the years is a single mom whose husband left her with six children. She was depressed and "had no place to look but up," Mike says.

In addition, she was having a hard time accepting help. But the lessons she learned in the study not only hit home with her but with her entire family.

This impact played out in a life-changing word to the mother from one of her children—a daughter. Frustrated by financial and emotional pressure, the mother told her family that they didn't need charity.

In response, the daughter said, "Mom, remember what charity means? Love." These words had a powerful effect on this single mom, who was able to accept the help that local believers were trying to give her.

Another couple taught by Mike and Liz were under tremendous financial pressure that was wearing heavily on the wife. She came to the class in tears, but as she and her husband moved through the material, she began to see light at the end of the tunnel. The tears have gone, and she's now looking at areas in which she can cut back and find extra money to put toward two major debts.

Freedom to serve

For Liz and Mike themselves, the benefits of following God's financial principles include being able to give when God places opportunities in their path. The beneficiaries of this giving have included ministries, a church that needed help with a building program, and a single mom, to whom they provided food and financial help for more than a year.

"Going through this Bible study series, and really studying what God's Word says about finances, has made the biggest difference in our lives in a practical sense and, I believe, in our relationship with the Lord," Mike says. "It's hard to express the influence that Larry Burkett has had on our marriage and on our finances over the past 18 years, but it has been dramatic.

"It is our prayer that Larry's teachings and materials would continue to be used throughout the world to bless God's people. It's exciting to see the changes in people's lives as a result of these materials. They're positive changes, and they're lifelong changes as well."

Sign Post

Lives are changed when the truth of God's Word is taught. People who have no hope regain the hope that God gives, as we help others through life's problems.

"But remember the Lord your God, for it is he who gives you the ability to produce wealth, and so confirms his covenant, which he swore to your forefathers, as it is today" *(Deuteronomy 8:18).*

The Source of Hope:

Waldinei and Luciany Bueno

By Waldinei Bueno

MY NAME IS WALDINEI, my wife is Luciany, and we have three children: Isabela, Leticia, and Gabriel.

We moved to Pompeia [Brazil] in January of 2002, up to our ears in debt that we had had for many years.

God really worked miracles in our lives. We were unemployed, and when we arrived in Pompeia, I was invited to work in shipping at the National Office of the Nova Shalom Association. Luciany was invited to teach at the school.

We heard about the Crown course, but we thought we would only be able to take it the following year. But God knew our needs. We were invited to be in the first group.

We have lived on the basis of postdated checks, loans, and investing in deals that never worked out.

Philippians 4:11-12 says, *"I have learned to be content in whatever circumstances I am. I know how to get along with humble means, and I also know how to live in prosperity."* But those verses were never a reality in my life.

Waldinei and Luciany Bueno with their children, Isabela, Leticia, and Gabriel.

I was dominated by ambition because the desire to become rich was very strong in my life. I never planned anything and did whatever I felt like doing without considering the consequences and without accepting advice.

After studying the biblical principles presented in the Crown small group study, my mind and heart were opened for the beginning of a transformation.

For the first time in our lives, we decided to get out of debt and never charge anything. We are paying off all of our debts one by one.

We had a car that had been financed, and we decided to return the car to the place we bought it. The funny thing was that no one wanted to take it back.

They all thought it was strange that someone would decide to take the loss of all the payments already made in order to get out of the remaining debt.

Without the car, my wife began to go to work by bicycle (borrowed). One dark morning, on the way to work in the cold, the Lord spoke to her heart. He told her that in the midst of all her difficulties, He wanted to teach her as He had the apostle Paul, who wrote, *"I have learned to be content in whatever circumstances I am."*

God taught us that He supplies all of our needs, but our dreams and the acquisition of superfluous things will come about if it is His will.

And this demonstrates how much the Lord Jesus wants us to trust in and depend on Him.

We have taught our children to depend on God, praying for our needs to be met, and we are teaching them to manage their money according to God's patterns. They are learning to give, save, and spend.

The lesson that impacted my life the most was the one on eternity. I discovered that being rich and getting everything I wanted would get me nowhere because this life is so very short!

Sign Post

 This life is very short compared to eternity. Spending time in this life in acquiring things will not help us when we enter eternity. All that we have done for the Kingdom of God will.

"Do not store up for yourselves treasures on earth, where moth and rust destroy, and where thieves break in and steal. But store up for yourselves treasures in heaven, where moth and rust do not destroy, and where thieves do not break in and steal. For where your treasure is, there your heart will be also" (*Matthew 6:19-21*).

Phil Drake's company took on the leadership role in developing the
latest version of the Money Matters software that Crown has sold for
years.

From Bankruptcy to Blessing:

The Story of Phil Drake

GROWING UP IN FRANKLIN, North Carolina, Phil Drake spent each spring as a "tax season orphan." His dad, who opened an accounting practice in Franklin in 1954, was tied up with the heavy paperwork of preparing tax returns in the pre-computer days. During these times, Phil stayed—and worked hard—on his grandparents' farm.

As a young adult, he left rural life and entered the teaching field in Greenville, South Carolina.

After three years, he and his wife, Sharon, became homesick and moved back to Franklin to be with their families, but Phil was unable to find a teaching job. He went to work in his dad's accounting practice, and the stage was set for the amazing events that would shape his life.

On the edge of a new concept

The year was 1976. Phil's dad was using a pencil to do his work, which he handed to his secretary, who then typed everything on carbon paper. "I started shopping for a computer," Phil says. "I was going to automate our practice."

In those days, there were no computer superstores, so Phil had to deal with an IBM salesman. In addition, computers had limited capabilities and were very expensive. For a machine with just 16 kilobytes of memory and a four-inch screen, Phil paid a whopping $22,000.

Yet, it was the latest technology—the first IBM computer that didn't have to be kept in a special air conditioned room.

It was at this point that Phil's natural giftedness with software began to shine.

He created tax processing programs for the new computer, and when the IBM salesman made a follow-up visit, he asked Phil to travel with him and sell his software.

Shock and surrender

"I was a Christian, but my mentality in those days was that God helps those who help themselves. I thought I was supposed to do everything on my own and call on God only when I got into trouble. I told Sharon I would be a millionaire by age 30, but God chose that age for me to be bankrupt.

"We had grown too fast and added employees, and we owed a lot of payroll taxes. The IRS closed our business in 1981, and we ended up in Chapter 11 bankruptcy. Our debt was six times our annual gross income, and the bankruptcy court determined we had the ability to pay only 20 percent of our debt."

Since the late 1970s, Phil had been listening to Larry Burkett on WLFJ in Greenville. He'd heard Larry talk about paying back 100 percent after a bankruptcy, and he and Sharon decided they wanted to honor the Lord by repaying everything they owed—however long it took.

"I told God I had messed up, and I started relying on Him," Phil says. "We paid off all our debts by 1987, only six years later. And since the bankruptcy, God has blessed what we've done."

A harvest of blessings

In the world of tax and accounting software, God placed Phil in the right place at the right time. The IRS began doing a pilot program for electronic filing in 1985, and it chose three test areas, one of which was Raleigh-Durham, North Carolina.

Three of Phil's customers were there. They asked him to help them with the pilot program, and they ended up doing about 25 percent of all the electronic filing done in the country that year.

They convinced Phil that this new concept had great potential, and he began to focus on electronic filing for the federal government and state governments.

Today, Drake Software serves tax preparers all over the country. It was involved in the processing of five million federal returns in 2004, as well as state returns.

But God's blessings on Phil have gone far beyond his software company, which employs about 350 people. Currently, he operates about a dozen businesses in Macon County, North Carolina, including a Christian bookstore and a Christian radio station.

The last business he opened is a family entertainment center called "The Factory." It's housed in a former Burlington Industries sewing plant where his mother worked in the 1950s.

Phil took the factory where his mother worked and turned it into a family entertainment center with attractions for adults as well as children.

Originally, Phil thought about using the building for office space, but he determined that Franklin needed a place where the entire family could go.

The Factory offers activities for kids like laser tag, batting cages, and bowling. It also offers a variety of food, including an upscale restaurant for parents.

"I wanted a place where parents could have a nice meal and their kids could have cheese toast and applesauce," Phil says.

He honors the Lord's Day by closing the business on Sundays, when he and Sharon lead praise and worship during one of the morning services at the First Alliance Church of Franklin.

A matter of stewardship

Phil says he's thankful for a wife who "kept me in line when I didn't want to be in line."

All of his three children are Christians, and he now has the privilege of being a spiritual mentor for his grandchildren.

But Phil sees his responsibility to influence others as going beyond his family, and the bookstore, radio station, and entertainment center are part of his efforts to influence the culture in Franklin.

Beyond his hometown, Phil is supporting organizations like Crown, Family Research Council, Compassion International, and Focus on the Family, which have the means to influence the culture in other places.

"I feel called to be a businessman," he says. "And I'm trying to use the resources God has entrusted to me to take back the culture, which has muddied the difference between right and wrong.

"When I get to heaven, God won't ask me how much money I made. He'll ask me how I used the money and who I brought with me. I want to bring people with me, and to do that, I have to be a good steward."

Sign Post

A good businessman uses the resources with which God has blessed him to affect the culture in which God has placed him, affecting those around him and those with whom he does business.

"His master replied, 'Well done, good and faithful servant! You have been faithful with a few things; I will put you in charge of many things. Come and share your master's happiness!'" (Matthew 25:21).

One blessing of being financially free is that Kevin can set aside Thursdays to do budget counseling based on God's financial principles.

A Jaguar, a Radio, and Gardening Shoes:

Kevin Cross

"IT'S AMAZING HOW GOD uses any medium to get your attention, even listening to the radio in someone else's car for just a couple of minutes," says Kevin Cross. "But all He needs is one moment to really change a person's heart."

Kevin's change of heart occurred when he reached the bottom—spiritually, emotionally, and financially—as a young man trying to survive in south Florida in the late 1980s.

Just a few years before, at age 19, he'd been awarded a scholarship to law school that covered half of his expenses. But instead of making him thankful, the scholarship fed his thinking that he was the "boy wonder."

He began using credit cards recklessly, adding to the student loan debt he'd incurred to pay the other half of his college expenses. He also violated school policies by taking money to do homework assignments for other students.

His debt continued climbing until it reached $100,000. After one year in law school, he was asked to take a leave of absence—because of legal troubles—and not come back until those troubles were cleared up. Then, to add to his emotional pain, the girl in his life dumped him.

Life in the pits

"I found myself at the bottom rung of life," Kevin says. "I got a day job, but the income only covered the minimum payments on my credit cards. I had to find a night job to take care of food and other living expenses."

Kevin applied for a job delivering pizzas but didn't have adequate insurance on his car. "I'd gone from being the 'boy wonder' to getting denied employment at Pizza Hut," he says. "But it was all part of God's plan, because He had to get hold of my life." One job Kevin did qualify for was valet parking, which required him to wear a uniform, including black Reebok tennis shoes that he had to buy for himself—at a cost of $50.

It seemed like an impossible sum to a young man who was basically destitute and had maxed out his credit cards. So, Kevin went to a local discount store and found a pair of black ladies' gardening shoes for $5.99.

"I thought, man, this is so humiliating, but I could afford them," he says. "The problem was they had white bands around them, which my manager wouldn't allow. So, I took a black marker and covered up the bands. The marker wasn't permanent, so I had to keep it in my pocket. Whenever I scuffed the shoes and the white showed through, I had to paint them again so my manager wouldn't send me home."

A lesson in God's economics

One night, a local newscaster drove up in a Jaguar, and Kevin was assigned to park the car. Unaware that the engine was still running, he turned the key, causing the starter to grind. The newscaster turned in his direction.

"If looks could kill, I wouldn't be here today," Kevin says. "It was so embarrassing, but before I could be kicked out of the car, I sped away.

"I thought, 'Oh Lord, I'm a mess. I'm at the lowest point. I can't even drive a car.' "

Kevin had been raised in a Christian home, and as a boy he'd accepted Christ as his Savior. He had drifted far from his spiritual upbringing, but in an effort to find his way back to God, he was listening to Miami's only Christian radio station.

Like the other young men he worked with, Kevin had a habit of changing the channel on the radios of the cars he parked. He turned the dial to the Christian radio station while he was parking the Jaguar, and the voice he heard was that of Larry Burkett.

"Larry was talking about how God owns it all and how we are just stewards, managers, of what God entrusts to us," Kevin says. "He said most of us are poor managers, and I thought, 'Man, I'm such a poor manager. I've mismanaged and mishandled God's resources. Everything He's given to me, everything He's put in my trust, I've squandered.' "

It was then that Kevin's present situation became a striking illustration of Larry's words. He was driving a car that belonged to someone else. Even the bowtie on his neck belonged to the parking company. He didn't own anything, and even though he'd paid for the ladies' gardening shoes, he certainly wasn't going to claim them as his own.

He prayed, "God, if you could ever use a guy who's made so many mistakes—who's had to learn the hard way after you've given him so many chances—if you could use somebody like that, I'm your man."

Applying the truth

Eager to learn what the Bible said about money, Kevin made numerous calls to Gainesville, Georgia, asking for every free item offered by Larry Burkett's ministry. "If Christian

Financial Concepts had had caller ID in those days, they probably would have blocked my calls," he says. "From that day forward, I made a covenant with God to not only get out of debt and practice His financial principles but to surrender my heart to Him.

"Implementing the principles was very important, but the big victory was when I surrendered my heart, because then, God could do some great things through me."

Kevin began working to get out of debt, and in 1990 he became a financial lay counselor, hoping to steer other people away from the problems he'd experienced himself.

A new girl, Stephanie, came into his life, and he made a covenant with her not to be married until he had paid off all his debt. That didn't happen until four years later, on July 3, 1993, one month after he'd made the last payment on his student loan.

For the next four years after that, Kevin and Stephanie lived off his income and saved hers, until they were able to make a 50-percent down payment on a house. In another four years they had completely paid off their mortgage.

By this time, Kevin had a bachelor's degree in accounting. He returned to school, earned a master's degree in taxation, and became an Enrolled Agent and Certified Public Accountant.

He now operates a CPA practice with four other people, and because he is financially free, he takes off every Thursday to do pro bono financial counseling.

Since the late 1990s, he has also served with Crown Financial Ministries as a seminar instructor, and recently he taught his first counselor training workshop.

He jokes that most of the people he counsels haven't failed as much as he did. "It offers them great hope," he says. "They know they can definitely get out from where they are.

"Some counselees want to know why I'm doing this for free. 'What's your motivation?' they ask. I tell them to stick with their current tax preparer, that I'm not trying to earn their business.

"I tell them I simply want to show people that their lives can go from hopelessness to great hope. And, if I can play even a small role in that, I have my reward.

"The wonderful blessing of seeing lives changed is incredible. It's better than being on the 50-yard line of any Super Bowl, and that, alone, is plenty of motivation."

Sign Post

 We have to face the truth about our problems before we can change things. We confess to the Lord that we have missed it (sinned) and ask Him to forgive us. He will, and He'll show us how to do it right.

"If we confess our sins, he is faithful and just and will forgive us our sins and purify us from all unrighteousness. If we claim we have not sinned, we make him out to be a liar and his word has no place in our lives" (1 John 1:9-10).

Free to Serve:
Jess and Angela Correll

WHEN JESS CORRELL WAS 19 and his brother was 17, they made it their goal to become the richest men in Kentucky.

Their father, an entrepreneur, had been involved in real estate, and after college, Jess and his brother tried a couple of small ventures in timberland. But the high interest rates of the early 1980s devastated the real estate market.

"We were looking for something else to do, and we found a bank that was having some financial problems," Jess says. "We learned that if banks were in trouble, they were relatively easy to buy. So, when I was about 25 years old, we bought the Lincoln County National Bank in Stanford, Kentucky."

Remembering their goal to become rich, the Correll brothers "pursued it with a vengeance," Jess says. "We acquired a bank or a company every two years."

However, success came at a price, and Jess' marriage ended in divorce. "I worked too hard," he says, "and I was too single-minded and focused.

"Today, I see that how you become successful is just as important as how successful you become. I didn't see that in those days.

"I've learned more from failures in my life than I have from successes, and you make a lot better decisions after you fail."

Seeing money the right way

Today, Jess realizes that when it came to money, he didn't have a proper perspective—God's perspective.

During this time, Lyston Peebles, a former Crown area director, began encouraging him to take the ministry's small group study.

"I really wasn't interested in the study," Jess says. "I told Lyston that I needed help in every area of my life but money.

"He said, 'Jessie, anybody who's stupid enough to say that really needs to go through the study.' "

Trusting his friend's advice, Jess and the top five officers in his banking company went through the small group study.

It was the late 1980s, and at the time, Jess and his brother were about $20 million in debt.

The magnitude of that obligation weighed heavily upon him. "I could tell you what the daily interest accrual was, and it was in the thousands of dollars per day," he says. "Interest rates in those days weren't in the low single digits, they were 10 percent to 12 percent."

After completing the Crown study, the brothers made a commitment to stop expanding, get control of their spending, and start paying down their debt.

They became debt free in only five years, and if they incur any debt today, it is only short term.

Their banking company has grown to 24 locations in Kentucky and about $750 million in assets.

Combined with a life insurance company that they own in Springfield, Illinois, their business assets total about $1 billion.

Doing business a different way

During the years they were living at home, Jess and his brother watched their father faithfully tithe.

They also tithed based on their after-tax income, but as they paid off their debt, they began tithing based on their pre-tax income and have been doing so ever since.

Jess says giving has been fun since he learned God's financial principles, and today he gives a large percentage of his income beyond the tithe.

In addition, the Correll's banking company has a foundation that gives away 10 percent of pre-tax earnings—a key advantage of being debt free.

Another practice that the Corrells instituted after the small group study was accountability.

"A Christian friend of ours meets with us every year, and we show him everything that we've earned and spent," Jess says. "We get his approval before we commit more than $10,000 to any particular expenditure.

"We share our time and money goals for the following year with him, and he makes sure we're spending the right amount of dollars and hours on certain things—not too much, not too little."

"[Angie] is an absolute partner in every way. She's my closest adviser, and we don't make significant giving decisions without each other's opinion."

Why undergo such scrutiny? Because "success equals influence," Jess says. And in light of his company's size, he feels responsible for using the influence God has entrusted to him in the right way.

The gift of an excellent wife

Following his divorce, Jess remained single for five years before marrying his wife, Angela. He views her as a gift from God and likens her to the example of a good wife in Proverbs 31:10, *"An excellent wife, who can find? For her worth is far above jewels."*

"She is an absolute partner in every way," he says. "She's my closest adviser, and we don't make significant giving decisions without each other's opinion. Most of the time we pray individually about how much to give to a particular organization, and generally, we come up with the same amount to give. It's a confirmation of who we should be supporting and how much we should be giving them."

Before marrying Jess, Angela managed her finances well. Still, Jess wanted her to experience the small group study because it had been a blessing to him. When Angela, a writer, completed the study, she summarized the principles taught by Crown:
- debt is bad,
- saving is good,
- giving is fun, and
- stuff is meaningless.

"That perspective on debt is quite different from the way it is in America today," Jess says. "Fifty years ago, people did think debt was bad. Today, they see it as just a tool for acquiring things. The problem is, it's a tool that can hurt you."

Co-laboring with crown

Just as he benefited from Crown, Jess wants to see others receive the same benefits. For that reason, he has become active in Crown by sharing its teachings with his family, by serving on the ministry's board of directors, and by funding its work.

"Recently, I've had the joy of seeing Crown's impact on our son," Jess says. "He led several small group studies during a two-year period at a summer horse camp. It was there that he met his wife, and now the two of them are going to India for a year to help with a school for street children.

"Crown is the number one ministry that our foundation supports. I'm impressed by the fact that Crown's cofounder, Howard Dayton, is humble, focused, and takes no salary from the ministry. I'm impressed by the leaders of the ministry and by the people who work there.

"That's why investing in Crown is like buying Microsoft 10 years ago for a penny a share. It's an excellent investment with a huge impact."

Sign Post

How you become successful is as important as how successful you become. Following God's principles and laws produces fruits of righteousness that are everlasting.

"And this is my prayer: that your love may abound more and more in knowledge and depth of insight, so that you may be able to discern what is best and may be pure and blameless until the day of Christ, filled with the fruit of righteousness that comes through Jesus Christ—to the glory and praise of God" (Philippians 1:9-11).

Patrick and Mary's journey to the mission field included a stop at a train station near Amsterdam with their three children (left to right): Julia, Sophie, and Aidan.

On "The Lost Continent:"

Patrick and Mary DeMuth

THE COBBLED STREETS OF PARIS have invited countless American couples vacationing there to return. Adorned with beautiful lights, the city of art and romance is one of the world's top tourism destinations.

Four years ago, Patrick DeMuth took his wife, Mary, on a surprise trip to Paris to celebrate their 10th anniversary.

Now they're back in France, but unlike most couples, they haven't returned as tourists.

During their anniversary trip to Paris, the couple saw the tremendous spiritual need in Europe, which missiologists now call "The Lost Continent."

"We were endeavoring to be church planters somewhere in the world," Mary says, "and we realized France is where we needed to be."

More than 99 percent of France's population is unchurched. And among the country's 38,000 towns, 36,000 have no resident evangelical outreach.

The DeMuths moved to France from Dallas, Texas in August 2004. Adjusting to life in their new home has been difficult, especially for their three children: Sophie, 11; Aidan, 8; and Julia, 6.

They expected most of the lessons in Sophie's international school to be delivered in English. Instead, they're primarily in French, which has made her efforts to learn more difficult.

"Sophie met a Christian girl the first day of school, and they've become inseparable," Mary says. "It's hard to find Christians around here, so I'm glad she found a friend."

Aidan and Julia are attending a French public school, where the teaching methods are different from those in the states. Both kids miss their friends in Dallas.

A financial foundation

For Patrick and Mary, seeing the struggles and tears of their children has been tough. Transitioning from jobs and salaries to depending on gifts from donors could be adding even more stress to their lives, but financial stewardship is one of the strongest areas of their relationship. That's very important considering they're in southern France, where the cost of living is among the highest in the world.

The couple were married in December 1990, and one month before they said their vows they developed a budget based on Larry Burkett's book, *The Complete Financial Guide for Young Couples*. They have been Crown outreach partners for years.

"I had a small student loan and Patrick had a fairly hefty one, so we used my income as a schoolteacher to pay all that off within about a year and a half," Mary says. "We used the rest of the money to save for a house, and with the exception of a van that we purchased on credit and paid off as quickly as we could, we've been debt free. This has been very helpful to us, especially as missionaries. We couldn't tolerate debt in our budget right now."

Mary says French believers have not yet been taught the importance of giving to the Lord or His ownership of all things. So, the couple's outreach not only represents an opportunity to share the Gospel with the lost but to share biblical financial principles with fellow Christians.

"I love what Larry had to say about God not being able to entrust us with higher things if He first could not entrust us with money," Mary says. "When we've taken spiritual gift inventories in the past, Patrick and I have both scored high on giving, but we believe that all Christians should score high in this area. If God has given us everything, then our purses should have holes that are always pouring out to other people in need."

Church planting challenges

Patrick graduated from seminary in May 2004, and the church that he and Mary are beginning to plant in southern France has a core group of about 15 French believers plus two other American families. Another three American families are expected to join them within a year.

The DeMuths are working with Christian Associates International, whose goal is to plant high-impact churches among postmodern Europeans.

Patrick and Mary, along with their team, are targeting a strategic area outside of Nice called Sophia Antipolis, an area where many international corporations' headquarters are located.

"It's the Silicon Valley of Europe," Patrick says. "Many people who live and work here do so to advance their careers, leaving family and all attachments behind. If I were to sum up the strongest spiritual reality here, it's loneliness. We believe that God desires to build His church here, to build a true community of faith for those who have never had one."

Currently, the DeMuths don't have a church building and are meeting in homes. One of their challenges is to make the church a nonprofit entity capable of receiving donations. Then, they'll be able to tithe to the church and begin building a reserve for renting or acquiring a building.

One ray of hope for a building came from the director of Sophie's international school, which has just opened a new high school facility that has a large auditorium and good parking, something that's hard to come by in France.

The DeMuths in Antibes, a harbor town in southeastern France.

Patrick was encouraged when the director noted the need for a church in his community and offered to help Patrick and Mary obtain their nonprofit status.

A matter of faith

When Patrick and Mary first settled in France and looked at their donations, they were less than 50 percent supported. "Part of me panicked," Mary says. "How could we live on that? I asked, 'Lord, what are you doing?' Then, I reevaluated and remembered. God had been utterly faithful to us in the past. Why wouldn't He be faithful today?"

During the past four years, Patrick and Mary have learned to live on a sporadic, transient income.

As a seminary student in Dallas, he went seven months with no regular income. The couple depended on their savings, and just when they were about to run out of money, Patrick received a good offer for contract work.

"We learned to budget so that our down months were fed by our up months," Mary says. "After four years of seminary, by God's provision, Patrick graduated with a Master of Theology degree and no debt."

Despite the shortage of support when they first arrived in France, Patrick and Mary chose to give to the Lord as usual. The last day of the month, another support update showed them getting closer to their goal.

An additional blessing for the DeMuths is that a book written by Mary, *Ordinary Mom, Extraordinary God*, was released by Harvest House in February 2005. Another of her books, also on parenting, was due to be released by Waterbrook in 2005.

Although France has very little Christian foundation on which Patrick and Mary can launch their ministry, she is encouraged by the words of the apostle Paul. "And thus I aspired to preach the gospel, not where Christ was already named, so that I would not build on another man's foundation; but as it is written, 'They who had no news of Him shall see, and they who have not heard shall understand'" (Romans 15:20-21).

"Our fervent prayer," Mary says, "is that Christ will once again be named in Europe."

Mary's Web site (www.relevantprose.com) has updates on her family's life in France. For daily musings on her family's life in France, visit her blog (www.relevantblog.blog-spot.com). Patrick's blog (www.emergenteuropechurch.blogspot.com) discusses emergent church planting in Europe.

Sign Post

Learn to budget even if you have no regular income. Save during times of plenty so there will be sufficiency in times of lack.

"Ants are creatures of little strength, yet they store up their food in the summer" (Proverbs 30:25).

A Divine Payoff:

Gaylyn and Jo Lynn Bright

JO LYNN BRIGHT had her first experience with borrowing at age 17, when she obtained a credit card from a local department store. On its own, the card might not have been a serious threat. But by the time Jo Lynn graduated from college, she was carrying several cards in her wallet, and she continued that practice right into her marriage, at the age of 34.

Both she and her husband, Gaylyn, who was 43 at the time, had been very involved with their careers and had remained single. But unlike her, he had not acquired credit cards until later in life.

"He was glad of that," Jo Lynn says. "But then I taught him how to be the king, because I was the queen of credit cards. We both had good jobs, but we were only making the minimum credit card payments."

Following their marriage in 1996, Gaylyn and Jo Lynn decided that she would be the bookkeeper. It was at that point that she came face to face with the difficulty of managing payments on some 15 cards she and her husband were using.

The issue wasn't a lack of money to make the payments, it was the organizational nightmare of keeping up with so many billing schedules plus making house payments, car

Once burdened with tens of thousands of dollar's worth of credit card debt, Gaylyn and Jo Lynn Bright now know the feeling of peace that comes with being debt free.

payments, payments to utilities, buying groceries, and so forth. "It was a lot of check writing," Jo Lynn says.

For a long time, she had been listening to Larry Burkett on the radio and believed he had her best interests at heart. And, about three years into her marriage, Larry's teaching on the importance of eliminating debt finally convinced her of the need for her and Gaylyn to get control of their finances.

They had always tithed, even before they were married, but in the areas of credit and saving, they needed to make some adjustments.

Jo Lynn bought a copy of Larry's *How to Manage Your Money* workbook and reviewed it with Gaylyn. Then, they developed a plan for paying off their credit card debt.

Over a period of about four years, they followed Larry's advice to pay off small debts and then apply the monthly payments on those debts to pay off larger obligations.

Throughout the process, Jo Lynn kept detailed records of how much credit card debt they were eliminating, and when they made their final payment on the last remaining card, the total came to $65,814.

Sharing the good news

Among the organizations that Gaylyn and Jo Lynn supported was Crown Financial Ministries. They sent their gifts directly to Crown's home office, but they weren't aware that the ministry had representatives in their hometown of Wichita, Kansas.

A friend and coworker of Jo Lynn urged her and Gaylyn to take Crown's Adult Small Group Study and to also become small group leaders. The couple went through the training and were introduced to Crown's Kansas state director, Stu Ferrell.

Six months later, Stu invited Jo Lynn to serve on Crown's Wichita city team, a position she has held for a year and a half. In this role, she has been working to take Crown into the African-American community and to assist with leadership training.

From the very beginning, God has blessed Gaylyn and Jo Lynn as Crown small group leaders. The first class at their church filled up quickly, and in time, they had an opportunity to share Crown with most of their church's membership. Now, they're teaching people from other churches in their community.

The deceitfulness of debt

Unlike many people who've paid off large amounts of debt, Gaylyn and Jo Lynn were not experiencing serious marital problems. They were not having difficulty finding the money to make their payments. So, when they awoke to the danger of the financial obligations they held, they realized how deceiving debt can be.

"We weren't prepared for any kind of emergency, and if a financial crisis had occurred, we could have been in really bad trouble," Jo Lynn says. "I told Gaylyn that if one of us lost a job, we'd have to live with friends or family."

Jo Lynn notes that other people in debt must have a similar awakening before they take action. "People believe they can continue spending and that their jobs will go on forever," Jo Lynn says. "I realized I didn't want to live in that kind of bondage anymore. We've felt free knowing that our debt is paid off and that we're not enslaved to other people whom we don't even see."

Jo Lynn notes that the process of eliminating debt became a habit for her and Gaylyn, not just something that lasted a few months. As a result, they won't fall into their old practices.

Their inspiration during the time they were paying off their debt was the Week 8 memory verse in the Crown study: *"Steady plodding brings prosperity; hasty speculation brings poverty"* (Proverbs 21:5 TLB).

"We had to tell each other all the time, 'It's just steady plodding,' " Jo Lynn says. "And our prayer during the four years was, 'Lord, honor our efforts. We want to be obedient to what you're calling us to do.'

"I really believe God helped us eliminate our debt earlier than ever imagined. And, along with meeting all our needs, He even provided several of our wants during the payoff period. We still took vacations, we were able to give to others in need, we bought a car, and we were timely in our payment obligations.

"Great is His faithfulness toward those who completely trust in Him. We give Him all the credit for every dime He helped us pay off."

Sign Post

 Debt puts you in a place of unrest, knowing that you are so close to the edge that if anything goes wrong, you'll be in trouble. Taking control of this kind of debt brings refreshing relief.

"As the deer pants for streams of water, so my soul pants for you, O God" (Psalms 42:1).

Among the Crown resources that Dick and Nancy have introduced to the Assemblies of God is the eight-week series, *Discovering God's Way of Handling Money.*

From District to District:

Dick and Nancy Hall

WHEN DICK HALL first joined the financial services group of the Assemblies of God, he found that his coworkers were looking for help in the field of stewardship education. "Many pastors had called looking for resources," Dick says.

But even though the need was great, Dick's coworkers didn't want to reinvent the wheel.

If they could find existing resources to meet their denomination's needs, they would be willing to use those resources.

A solution to their need came when Howard Dayton addressed the denomination's stewardship and development conference on a Friday night in Phoenix, Arizona.

The following Saturday, Dick was part of a group of people who went through Crown's small group leader training.

His responsibility was stewardship education, which was initially limited to the denomination's stewardship will program, which he shared around the country with Assemblies of God churches.

Following the leader training session, he also took on the responsibility for introducing Crown to the denomination.

There was no manual to show him how to share Crown's resources with the denomination's 12,000 U.S. churches, which are located in 58 districts around the country.

So, after much prayer and consultation, he began sharing Crown's resources with district leaders and church leaders as God moved them to have an interest in what the ministry had to offer.

His training sessions have consisted of as many as 80 people at once, and he begins by sharing the denomination's stewardship will program on a Friday night. He follows this on Saturday with Crown small group leader training.

Meeting the demand

When Dick began offering Crown, he expected to do training in one district per month. And at that rate, it would have taken years for him to reach all 58 districts.

However, he ended up doing two trainings per month, and demand has been so strong that, in October 2005, he did training on four out of five weekends.

"We're seeing 30 to 40 people in most of our training sessions," Dick says. "I'm doing another session this weekend in southern California, where 50 people are signed up."

Dick's wife, Nancy, accompanies him on many of his trips and helps district workers with things like food for the events. In addition, she is a capable Crown leader.

"One day I came home and was very sick," Dick recalls. "It was Week 4 of our first Crown group, and our co-leader was traveling. Nancy told me I ought to go to bed, and I said, 'If I do that, who's going to lead the group?' She said, 'I will,' and she's being doing it ever since."

As with endeavor in Dick's life, Nancy, his wife of 42 years, has been involved with his effort to share Crown with all 58 U.S. districts of the Assemblies of God denomination.

"Nancy has been an integral part of everything I've done. When I was manager of governmental affairs for an electric utility company, she was always involved in the company's activities.

"When I was a city councilman, she was involved. We've been a team effort during our 42 years of marriage, and Crown is just another extension of that."

Seeing Crown for the first time

One of the most rewarding aspects of Dick's job is witnessing the positive effect that Crown has on people who are exposed to God's financial principles for the first time.

"The most frequent reaction I get is, 'I wish I'd known this 10, 20, or 30 years ago,' " Dick says, noting that most people understand tithing but are amazed to see all the other biblical teachings on managing money.

People also are amazed at the way that Howard Dayton's book, *Your Money Counts*, presents God's ownership of all things. People often say things like, "I always knew that God owned it all, but I never quite knew it the way Howard said it."

"I smile every time that happens, because it happens over and over again," Dick says. "People also comment on how well-organized the materials are and, particularly, how biblically-based they are."

Dick says he begins praying for each training session the day it is scheduled.

He trusts that each person who registers is sent by God, and each time the name of a new registrant is received, he prays for that individual.

A growing outreach

Along with stewardship will and small group training, Dick is also seeing a need for budget counselor training, and he's meeting that need with Crown's budget counselor training course.

Now, people within the Assemblies of God are desiring to use Crown's resources to provide stewardship training to groups like young couples and children.

In addition, the denomination has hired an individual to present stewardship will and Crown leader training to the Spanish-speaking community.

The Assemblies of God is the largest Pentecostal denomination, with 51 million members and adherents worldwide.

And Dick is working with Crown's international department to see how he can bring Crown's message to members of the denomination in other countries.

"Sharing Crown has been a tremendous blessing for us," Dick says. "We appreciate it so much, and the thing that makes it so nice is people's reception of the material.

"We've probably trained close to 1,500 leaders around the country, and it's a blessing every time we hear people tell how God has moved them to come to these training sessions. We're just very much in awe of what's happening."

Editor's note: The Assemblies of God is among a number of alliances that Crown has formed in order to reach more people with God's principles for handling money. If you are aware of another organization that might be interested in forming an alliance with Crown, contact Liz Hart at Lhart@crown.org.

Sign Post

Howard Dayton puts God's ownership on all things in a way that caused people to wonder why they had never seen that in the Word before.

"So we fix our eyes not on what is seen, but on what is unseen. For what is seen is temporary, but what is unseen is eternal" *(2 Corinthians 4:18).*

A Journey of Faith:
Glenn and Susan Preston

ALONG WITH BEING THE CREATOR and Owner of all things, God is ultimately in control of every event that occurs on the earth. In that light, He is more than capable of providing for our needs.

Jesus said, *"Do not worry then, saying, 'What will we eat?' or 'What will we drink?' or 'What will we wear for clothing?'...But seek first His kingdom and His righteousness, and all these things will be added to you"* (Matthew 6:33).

Glenn and Susan Preston of Oakwood, Georgia can attest to the reality of that promise. They are the parents of six children ranging in ages from 2 to 16 years, but only Glenn works full time.

First exposure to Crown
Early in his life, when he was living in Birmingham, Alabama, Glenn was introduced to the teachings of Larry Burkett by a coworker, Vicky Putman, and her husband Dennis.

"Dennis wanted her to stay home with the kids," Glenn says. "He had listened to Larry's tapes in the mid-1980s, and he became his family's sole provider. Dennis gave me a stack of Larry's tapes and explained the importance of living on a budget. He was living by those principles himself."

Unfortunately, Glenn wasn't completely ready to put Dennis' advice into practice. Not long after this, he married his wife Susan, and early in their marriage they had financial problems.

The couple moved to Auburn, Alabama, where he was going to attend graduate school and she planned to work full time. But six months after the wedding, Susan learned she was pregnant and had to stay home with their child.

Glenn earned money through a teaching assistantship while attending graduate school to study physical education. He also worked from 3 p.m. to 11 p.m. on Saturdays and Sundays at a local hospital.

"It wasn't the smartest way to do things," he says. "I should have gotten a full-time job and gone to school part time." However, God provided for the couple through a number of means, including help from their parents.

Crown for the second time

Glenn's physical education career eventually took him to North Georgia College and State University in Dahlonega, Georgia, where Don Delozier, an instructor for Crown, presented a seminar at his church.

Once again, Glenn was shown the need to handle his money according to God's financial principles.

He and Susan had a large amount of credit card debt, so he sought Don's help in developing a budget. "Don told us to be faithful and watch God bless," Glenn says, noting that he and Susan received an unexpected windfall that allowed them to completely repay their debts.

One benefit of having a dad who's a weight training coach is having your own personal trainer at home. Sixteen-year-old Andrew (right) learns from his dad's experience.

However, when Glenn moved into his current job as fitness center director and facilities coordinator at Gainesville College, he lost touch with his budget. He and Susan moved to Oakwood, Georgia, where the college is located, and their expenses changed. "I didn't update our budget," he says, "and our debt started mounting."

A third encounter with crown

Last year, Glenn went through Crown's small group study, which takes participants through a deep journey into God's Word.

"I had done the mechanical part," he says, "but the Scriptures made the difference. This time I got a heart transplant. I had never seen that the way you handle money affects your intimacy with Christ. Every day you're in the study, you're in the Scriptures, and the Scriptures will change your heart."

One portion of the study that impressed Susan was the chapter on work. She has since started a small home business selling gourmet foods, which gives her an occasional break and fellowship with other women. Susan is also teaching biblical financial principles to middle school girls at her church.

In late January, Glenn and Susan had the opportunity to tell people across the nation about the manner in which God has changed their finances. During a CBS special about growing national interest in the Bible's view on money, Crown Financial Ministries was featured. A CBS camera crew set up their equipment in the couple's home and allowed them to share their story.

"For Susan and me, Crown has been life-changing," Glenn says. "We appreciate the time and effort put into the resources Crown provides. We're grateful to Howard Dayton and to his business partner, Jim Seneff, for the effort they made to search the Scriptures and to discover all that God has to say about managing our money."

Sign Post

 Every day you are in the Word, the Word will change your heart. As you search the Word, you discover what God has in store for your life.

"Therefore, I urge you, brothers, in view of God's mercy, to offer your bodies as living sacrifices, holy and pleasing to God—

Pictured in the front row (left to right) are Gabriel, age 4 and Samuel, 5. In the back row (l-r) are Andrew, 16; Joshua, 14; Elisabeth, 12; Susan; and Glenn, holding two-year old Emma.

this is your spiritual act of worship. Do not conform any longer to the pattern of this world, but be transformed by the renewing of your mind. Then you will be able to test and approve what God's will is—his good, pleasing and perfect will" (Romans 12:1-2).

Three years ago, Tom was given the opportunity to reenter the dairy business, which has been a part of his life since he was a child.

Taking God at His Word:
Tom and Suzanne Blevins

IN TIMES OF GREAT DIFFICULTY, Christians are often tempted to compromise. Tom and Suzanne Blevins faced such a time several years ago, when his father's bankruptcy sent creditors to his door in search of repayment for an $800,000 debt.

Tom's attorney recommended that he also file bankruptcy. But he and Suzanne, who were in the midst of a Crown small group study, knew that God had a better plan for their lives.

"I was born and raised in the dairy business," Tom says, but due to financial distress, he and his dad sold their business to the Dairy Buyout Program in 1986.

Following the sale of the business, Tom's parents moved into a nearby town. He and Suzanne moved into his parents' house, and they worked about five years to try to hang on to the house and land.

The house measured about 2,000 square feet and had three bedrooms. It was comfortable for the couple's growing family of three children, but in 1993 it was sold through a foreclosure sale.

Seven years of perseverance

Tom and Suzanne moved into an apartment with one bedroom and a den. At the time, they had two small girls and a baby daughter.

To make matters worse, creditors began knocking on Tom's door because he was the only person they could pursue in hopes of repaying his father's $800,000 debt.

During their seven years in the apartment, the couple had a fourth daughter who was delivered with the help of a midwife because they had no health insurance at the time.

Tom originally signed a six-month lease on the apartment, figuring that he and his family would move on to more permanent living quarters in the near future.

"Our church was sponsoring some Crown classes," Tom says. "We signed up and were convicted immediately that we weren't going anywhere until we were debt free, and it ended up taking us seven years to do that."

Fortunately, Tom and Suzanne were not required to repay the entire $800,000 debt. Recognizing that he wasn't aware of everything going on in the business, some of the creditors wrote off the debt.

"A couple of them did not," Tom says. "My attorney told me on at least three occasions to just file bankruptcy and get it over with. And I said, 'I can't do that. I don't know how we're going to pay these guys back. I don't know what's going to happen, but we sit in these Bible studies and study Scripture, and I just don't think bankruptcy is biblical.' "

God's miraculous provision

During their first two years in the apartment, Tom says he and Suzanne received a lot of support from everyone. By the fourth year, a number of people were questioning their commitment.

However, the couple received a lot of support from their Crown class, and God provided for them in miraculous ways.

One night, while standing around a campfire with fellow church members, a woman asked about Suzanne's clothing budget because she always looked so "stunning."

But Tom estimates that during the time he and Suzanne lived in the apartment, she spent very little on clothes for herself and probably no more than $100 on clothes for their girls.

The family received gifts of clothing, and Suzanne bought clothes at yard sales.

Tom remembers one specific blouse-skirt outfit that cost his wife $1.10. One of the items sold for a dollar and the other sold for a dime.

Another miracle involved Tom's pickup truck. During the time he was in the apartment, he put his construction skills to work by building things like corrals, barns, and dairy equipment.

Pictured in the front row (left to right) are Anna, age 19; Katelyn, 12; and Laci, 16. In the back row are Suzanne, Tom, and Grace, 6.

His truck was vital to him, but the engine wore out, and replacing it was going to cost $1,200.

Believing he had no other choice, Tom planned to buy a new motor, but Suzanne urged him to stay within the limits of their budget and let God provide for this need. One night, when he returned home from playing basketball with some friends, he walked in and found his wife and daughters were overjoyed. "What in the world's going on?" he asked. They replied that someone called while he was away and gave them the money they needed to replace the engine.

A fresh start

Three years ago Tom was given the opportunity to be a partner in a 500-cow dairy with a man who already had the necessary equipment.

He's enjoying the work, and he and Suzanne are continuing to lead Crown small group studies.

They're both involved in the music ministry of their church and in the leadership of men's and women's groups.

Looking back, Tom says that during his sixth year in the apartment, there didn't seem to be a light at the end of the tunnel.

But God honored the couple's commitment and has tremendously blessed them during the past several years.

The events of Tom's life have left him in a position where he can identify with Mary as she saw the amazing things that were happening in Jesus' life.

The Bible says that as she observed these things, she *"pondered"* them in her heart (Luke 2:19 KJV).

As Tom looks back at all the miraculous things God did for him and for his family, he says he can relate to Mary's wonder.

Sign Post

 It is amazing to see the things that God does for those who trust in and rely on His word—those who take Him at His Word.

"Therefore the Lord, the God of Israel, declares: 'I promised that your house and your father's house would minister before me forever.' But now the Lord declares: 'Far be it from me! Those who honor me I will honor, but those who despise me will be disdained'" (1 Samuel 2:30).

Relying on the Lord:
Michael and Chris Parker

DURING THE SECOND WEEK of Crown's small group study, students memorize two of the most beautiful and inspiring verses found in the entire Word of God.

"Everything in the heavens and earth is yours, O Lord, and this is your kingdom. We adore you as being in control of everything. Riches and honor come from you alone, and you are the Ruler of all mankind; your hand controls power and might and it is at your discretion that men are made great and given strength" (1 Chronicles 29:11-12 TLB).

About two years ago, these verses had amazing implications for Michael Parker, pastor of student ministries at Grace Community Church in Tempe, Arizona, and for his wife, Chris.

Michael has seen God working throughout his entire life to lead him to the place where he is today. "God called me when I was in the eighth grade to be a youth pastor," he says. "There was something about my youth pastor's character in those days, and I wanted to be like him."

Although Michael was not a Christian at the time, he was pursuing his faith. He drifted a little from that goal when his

youth pastor was removed from his job. But he came to know
Christ as Savior in March 1989 at the age of 22, and he
immediately knew that God had been pursuing him for years,
seeking control of his life.

Following God's call

"I was a believer for about six months when I started
interacting with high school ministries," Michael says. "I really
believe God was calling me to this, and within a year of
becoming a believer I started discipling high school students
and watching God ignite their faith."

Michael decided to attend Bible college, and Chris was in
school at the same time. They were $300 short of what they
needed to survive every month, but God provided for their
needs.

"There would be food on our table," Michael says. "There
would be money for our car payment, and there would be
somebody fixing our car for free. God provided every month
in some miraculous way."

During this time, Michael and Chris learned an early
lesson about surrendering everything to God. They stopped
tithing, and the amazing blessings stopped coming. "When
we started tithing again, the blessings started coming again,"
Michael says. "It was a real eye-opener for us."

An introduction to Crown

About two years ago, the leadership at Grace Community
Church encouraged all the members to go through the
Crown study.

Like other families across the nation, some of the Parker's special memories are family vacations. By God's grace, two-year-old Cassidy was able to be part of this trip. Pictured (left to right) are Michael, Cassidy; Kendra, age 4; Jeremy, 7; Charis, 5; and Chris.

Michael and Chris joined a Crown group headed by Steve Vlahovich, the church's stewardship pastor. At the time, Chris was expecting their fourth child, a girl named Cassidy.

About 12 days before Cassidy's due date, Chris began having contractions. And when Cassidy was born, it was obvious something was wrong.

Her skin looked like a mixture of green and purple, and in just a few moments the nurses were rushing her to the neonatal intensive care unit at the hospital.

The problem was that Cassidy did not have enough blood in her body, and initially, the doctors had no idea why. Within an hour she received two blood transfusions, as well as tests.

"They discovered that she had been bleeding inside her mom," Michael says. "Somewhere in her umbilical cord there was a pinhole leak. But by the grace of God, she came 12 days early.

"We would have lost her if she had gone another 24 to 48 hours. We got to keep Cassidy, but there were about three days when her situation was up and down."

It was at this point that 1 Chronicles 29:11-12 began to take on a special meaning for Michael. Remembering that God was "in control of everything," he wrote the 11th verse on a card and placed it beside his struggling daughter.

"That's what we were clinging to," Michael says. "We knew that God was in absolute control of everything. We needed to trust Him, believe in Him, worship Him, and even adore Him through all of that. It wasn't that easy, but we knew that's what God wanted."

Within the next 48 hours, Cassidy became stronger. She suffered no brain damage or harm of any kind as a result of her experience.

"I look at her now and realize what we almost lost," Michael says. "It's just amazing to us."

Ministering to moms and kids

Today, Grace Community Church is still offering Crown classes on a regular basis. The church is also offering guidance on planned giving, which is another concept promoted by Crown.

Chris is working with young mothers in the church and offers parenting tips to a group of about 80 mothers. She's also mentoring about seven moms on Wednesday nights.

"That's her gift," Michael says. "She's a great mom, and the one compliment we get from so many people is how well-behaved our kids are and how well-adjusted they are. So, she wants to help other moms try to figure things out. It's not that we're perfect. We're not! But she's doing a great job at parenting."

The student ministry at Grace has boomed. God has placed large numbers of junior high and high school students in Michael's sphere of influence.

Each weekend he has the opportunity to interact with some 300 students and try to steer them toward the Lord. And, best of all, he's doing what he knows God called him to do at an early age.

Sign Post

 The Word of God produces wonderful results when applied to our everyday lives. His Word is the truth we can count on.

"He says, 'I will declare your name to my brothers; in the presence of the congregation I will sing your praises." And again, "I will put my trust in him.' And again he says, 'Here am I, and the children God has given me.' Since the children have flesh and blood, he too shared in their humanity so that by his death he might destroy him who holds the power of death—that is, the devil" (Hebrews 2:12-14).

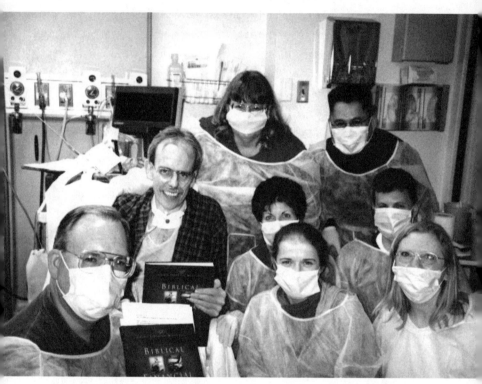

Pictured (front row, left to right) are co leader Marty Middleton, Linnea Diggle, Sue Middleton, (second row, left to right) co leader Mike Telfer (without mask), Cassie Elechicon, John Diggle, (third row, left to right) Debbie Telfer and Lem Elechicon. Group members not pictured are Bart and Gloria Moscarello and Dave and Joann Weretka.

A Surprise Visit:

The Miraculous Life of Mike Telfer

MANY PEOPLE MAY NOT KNOW that Charlotte Elliott, author of the song "Just as I Am," spent 52 years as an invalid. But although she was physically weak, God turned her into a spiritual giant. Her powerful song, written in 1836, is still a key component of church invitations around the country.

Mike Telfer of Plainfield, Illinois knows what it's like to be limited by illness, and like Charlotte Elliott, he has a desire for God to use him in a powerful way. That desire began to be fulfilled during the spring of 2004 through one of several Crown small groups sponsored by Harvest Baptist Church in Oswego, Illinois.

An amazing recovery

The story of how Mike got to this point begins in the summer of 1992, when he was diagnosed with cancer at age 34. "It was totally unexpected," he says. "I was a nonsmoker, I was athletic, but I was having terrible chest pains. It turned out to be a tumor to the thymus gland, which is outside the lung."

Along with two extensive surgeries and a long series of radiation treatments, Mike suffered from numerous complications.

As a result of the radiation and cancer surgeries, he had a tremendous amount of scar tissue that caused pressure on his heart and arteries. And in December 1995, he underwent quadruple heart bypass surgery.

"That was extraordinarily complicated," he says. "They brought in the best surgeon in the Midwest because of all the scar tissue." The surgeon completed the bypass, but only four months later the propensity of Mike's body to generate scar tissue rendered the bypass ineffective.

"They had to go in and attempt a second bypass," Mike says. "My cardiologist had to talk the surgeons into it. They didn't want to do it because of all the problems they knew they would face. But because of my age at the time—I was only 38—they decided they would attempt it."

In April 1996 the surgeons began the second bypass. Five hours later, Mike's wife Debbie received word that there had been severe complications.

Because of scar tissue, surgeons were unable to identify any of the structures in Mike's chest.

And when they tried to cut away part of that tissue, they cut a vein, which resulted in excessive bleeding.

The veins they had taken from Mike's leg in order to do the bypass ended up being used to fix the veins they had cut. Nothing was accomplished, and Mike was given one month to live.

Fellow believers rallied around Mike, praying around the clock. He became stronger, and although he wasn't able to return to work, he is able to do a lot of things that surprised a lot of people, like walking and talking.

Today, Mike has a pacemaker. He also has a ventilator in his home, but he only has to use it at night.

"I'm pretty much a medical miracle and a miracle of supernatural grace as well," he says. "The Lord was very merciful and gave me the impression that I was here for a reason. I still had something to accomplish."

An opportunity to serve

Mike's search for God's purpose in his life reached a high point when his church was visited by John Harper, a local director for Crown in Chicago.

"My career had been in the financial business," Mike says. "I investigated Crown very thoroughly, and when I found out that the co-leader's job is to facilitate, I thought, 'Maybe I could do this.'"

Following through on his desire, Mike became a co-leader with fellow church member Marty Middleton.

The group bonded instantly, and in the first week, Mike's prayer request was to complete his commitment to the group for the full 10 weeks of the small group study.

It was rare that he could go 10 weeks without being hospitalized or limited for a period of time.

A bump in the road

During the sixth week of the study, Mike developed a blood infection and was placed in intensive care at a local hospital. After a couple of days, he began to improve.

"I was a little upset that I was going to miss the Crown class," he says. "But Sue Middleton, Marty's wife, talked to my wife Debbie about having the class in the hospital room.

"It was an intensive care room. I was in isolation because my immune system was so weak. You couldn't even come into the room without putting on gloves, a mask, and a special gown. And, they usually let just two visitors in at a time."

However, Mike was what he calls a "frequent flyer" at the hospital. Everyone there knew him well, and when Debbie asked the administration about having the class in his room, they gave her permission, with limitations on noise and time.

Mike notes that Debbie has been a tremendous inspiration to him in his recovery.

"Her value is far beyond rubies," he says. "I was very touched when all these people started coming into the room for the class. I was released from the hospital two to three days later, and I was able to make it all 10 weeks, which was very important to me."

Future ministry opportunities

Mike kept close track of what happened in his Crown group, and during the 10 weeks there were 18 answers to prayer. In addition, members of the group have remained very close and still meet for fellowship once a month.

Today, Mike is looking at becoming a Crown budget counselor and leading another small group study.

"I think Crown is an extremely valuable course that is well thought out and designed," he says. "It gave me a very clear idea about what God expects from us regarding the other 90 percent of our money outside the tithe. And, it helped me focus on my heavenly treasure versus what I can accumulate on this earth.

"Crown has reinforced the power of prayer and has enabled Debbie and me to develop deep-seeded relationships with caring prayer partners. From a practical standpoint, it has enabled us to prioritize our spending and develop a clear plan for our financial future."

Sign Post

 God meets us where we are and has a plan for our lives, which will be revealed to us as we yield to His Word.

"But blessed is the man who trusts in the Lord, whose confidence is in him. He will be like a tree planted by the water that sends out its roots by the stream. It does not fear when heat comes; its leaves are always green. It has no worries in a year of drought and never fails to bear fruit" (Jeremiah 17:7-8).

Road Maps to Success:

Bobby and Claire Shoemaker

INFLUENCE. As we're thanking God for our blessings, it's something we should be careful not to overlook. The good influences in our lives help to shape our character, guide us away from decisions we'd later regret, lead us to Christ, and strengthen our walk with the Lord.

As he looks back over his life, Bobby Shoemaker can be thankful for many good influences, including Chick-fil-A, where he began working as a team member in 1984.

In those days, the company's stores were primarily found in the Southeast. But God has blessed the company, which is closed on Sundays in honor of the Lord's Day and now has stores all over the U.S.

Bobby's employment with Chick-fil-A placed him around a lot of Christians. And, at the age of 24, he accepted Christ as his Savior. He was led to the Lord by the father of a Chick-fil-A coworker.

"I didn't grow up in church, and I was skeptical of tithing," Bobby says. "But after I was saved, I was under the teaching of a man who addressed the subject of tithing and giving.

"He felt God was calling him to give 10 percent, and I felt challenged to do the same. I started giving one percent, and each month after that I increased my giving by one percent. In the tenth month, I wrote my first full 10 percent tithe check. The next day I began full-time employment with Chick-fil-A as an operator in their intern program. I also became engaged to my wife, Claire."

Claire grew up in a Christian home and is another one of the good influences in Bobby's life.

The couple have been married 12 years and have three children. They live in Gainesville, Georgia, where Bobby has operated the same Chick-fil-A store for nine years.

Blessed by God's Word

Although Bobby had made a commitment to tithe, he says he hadn't fully committed his finances to God. "I had a 90/10 thought process when it came to money," he says. "I didn't have any problem putting 10 percent in the offering plate, but I regarded the other 90 percent as mine to manage."

It was at this point that Bobby was introduced to another key influence in his life. He and Claire attend Lakewood Baptist Church in Gainesville, where fellow church member Robin Greene, an employee of Crown's home office, was helping to launch the ministry's small group studies.

Bobby and Claire signed up and, like so many other people, were deeply touched by Week 2 of the study and its memory verses: "Thine, O Lord, is the greatness, and the power, and the glory, and the victory, and the majesty: for all that is in the heaven and in the earth is thine; Thine is the kingdom, O Lord, and thou art exalted as head above all. Both riches and honour come of thee, and thou reignest over all: and in thine hand is power and jight; and in thine hand it

One of the Shoemaker's favorite pastimes is baseball. Bobby takes time out to practice with Caleb (left) and Brett.

is to make great, and to give strength unto all" (1 Chronicles 29:11-12).

Claire's sister embroidered a copy of those verses, which now hangs in a frame in the couple's home. "Just realizing that everything belongs to God really impacted us," Claire says. "We were giving, but seeing this truth helped us acknowledge that everything else belongs to God."

A company ideal

As they did in his personal finances, the Scriptures in the Crown study influenced Bobby's business finances as well.

He says one of the lines in Chick-fil-A's purpose statement talks about glorifying God by being a good steward of all He has entrusted to us.

For the Shoemakers, budgeting is a family affair. Pictured (left to right) are Claire; Amelia, 8 months; Caleb, 6; Brett, 9; and Bobby.

Another line talks about having a positive influence on everyone who comes in contact with Chick-fil-A.

Using the principles in the Crown study as a guide, Bobby looked at how to be a better steward of the Chick-fil-A store God had entrusted to him.

"We looked at each cost and made sure we were doing the best job of managing the profits and losses," he says. "The result was a dramatic increase in the profitability of the business."

The next generation

Since going through Crown, Bobby and Claire have been involved in leading studies at Lakewood. They're also getting an early start on teaching their children how to handle money God's way.

Brett and Caleb each has a giving bank, and both have allowances that they're learning to manage. Tithing is part of the boys' budgets, and they're learning the practice of saving by setting aside money over time for the things they want.

When a tsunami destroyed coastal areas in the Indian Ocean last year, Bobby and Claire turned the event into a learning project in which the boys set aside a portion of their money to contribute to relief efforts.

This teaching, as well as Bobby and Claire's success in personal and business budgeting, is a part of the overall financial structure that they now have in place.

"One of the things we always say when we're doing a Crown orientation at church is that during the first seven years of our marriage, Claire and I tried budgeting," Bobby says. "I'm pretty savvy with computers and numbers, but budgeting in our marriage wasn't working.

"The accountability piece of Crown over a 10-week period was a major factor for us.

"When we landed in a Crown study and began to work within the confines of our small group's accountability, we were successful at budgeting and got out of debt."

Sign Post

 God wants us to be 100 percent with Him. Not 10 percent on Sunday and 90 percent the rest of the week. All that we are and all that we have are His and we can trust that He will take care of us.

"Command those who are rich in this present world not to be arrogant nor to put their hope in wealth, which is so uncertain, but to put their hope in God, who richly provides us with everything for our enjoyment. Command them to do good, to be rich in good deeds, and to be generous and willing to share. In this way they will lay up treasure for themselves as a firm foundation for the coming age, so that they may take hold of the life that is truly life" (1 Timothy 6:17-19).

Beyond Medicine:
Buck, Andrea, and Ben Stephens

"IT'S BEEN AN INCREDIBLE FAITH WALK," says
Buck Stephens about the last two years. But he is quick to
note, "Faith walks are always lonely."

Shocking news can make us feel alone, and the news that
Buck and his wife, Andrea, received on May 1, 2003 was no
exception. Their 17-year-old son, Ben, was diagnosed with
end-stage kidney failure, although he showed no signs of
illness.

Ben's doctor predicted he would be on dialysis by July.
His kidneys were only functioning at 14 percent of their
capacity, and he needed a transplant right away.

Following the doctor's announcement, Buck was sitting
there praying, "Lord, give me something to say." But he wasn't
getting anything.

A statement of faith

Described by Buck as an "incredibly committed believer,"
Ben had been active in Crown with his dad since 1998. The
two traveled together to churches, conferences, and

conventions. Ben became a site manager for his dad's weekend speaking engagements, which have developed into city-wide conferences involving multiple churches.

After hearing his diagnosis, Ben looked at the doctor and said, "I respect you. I hear what you're saying, but I'm going to say it like the Apostle Paul said it: None of these things move me. I'm not going to let my circumstances move my faith. I'm going to let my faith move my circumstances. I'm believing that I won't need this transplant."

Ben's doctors put him on the fast track toward a kidney transplant and initiated testing at Saint Barnabas Hospital in New Jersey. The tests showed that Buck was a better than average donor for his son's needs. Still, the family continued looking for a miracle.

"We said, 'God, we don't believe this is Your best,' and we began asking other people to join us in praying," Buck says. "I had spoken at close to 50 churches that previous year, and people in those churches began calling on the Lord. I received so many contacts that I couldn't respond to all of them. So, I had to send out e-mail updates to large numbers of people at one time."

An unusual deliverance
About a week and a half before Ben's scheduled surgery, which was September 29, 2003, he was not on dialysis. In fact, his condition had improved.

And when Buck finished his pre-surgery testing, he received startling news. There was a suspicious lump in his lung that showed signs of calcification, meaning that cancer might be present.

Buck has been blessed to speak at large gatherings of people at churches in the Northeast.

Buck laughed as the doctor looked at him strangely. "I was wondering how the Lord was going to postpone this surgery," he said. He walked out of the room, and in the hall he met a Christian friend he hadn't seen in a long time. He explained what was happening, and his friend agreed with him in prayer that the lump would prove to be nothing serious and that Ben would be healed.

The surgery was canceled and rescheduled for 30 days later, in October. In the meantime, the doctors did further testing on Buck. In two to three weeks, another MRI showed that the lump was looking more like scar tissue and that the calcification was no longer there.

"They were very baffled by this and told me the next step was up to me," Buck says. "I told them that we would move forward, but we continued to pray for a miracle."

The lump in Buck's lung eventually disappeared completely. It is the second medical miracle in his life. In 1995, an abscess on his colon ruptured, and doctors predicted he would not make it through the night.

During the month that followed, including a week on a ventilator in intensive care, Buck says he received a great deal of wisdom and guidance from the Lord. His ideas about finances and business changed, and today, his business is run according to God's principles and provides the funding for his ministry activities.

A voice from Africa

About a week before the rescheduled transplant surgery in October, Buck received a call from a friend in the medical field who had traveled with Ben and him to Kenya, where they had helped to establish a clinic.

The friend had heard about Ben's illness and informed Buck that he and Ben may have contracted a parasite in Kenya that attacks the kidneys.

The transplant surgery was canceled again and tests on Ben and Buck showed they did not currently have the parasite.

However, it was possible that the parasite had infected them and that their immune systems had destroyed it.

At this point, Buck, Andrea, and Ben sat down and reviewed the events of the past few months. Recognizing that the Lord had canceled the surgery twice, they decided to forget the transplant and trust God for a miracle.

Ben graduated from high school last year and has since moved from his home state of New York to Tulsa, Oklahoma, where he attends Oral Roberts University. He is pursuing a degree in mass media communications at ORU, where he was given the opportunity to work as an audio assistant for live Christian television. Within two weeks he became the floor audio man for various shows.

He has a Christian doctor in Tulsa who put him through some follow-up tests in April 2005 that showed his kidneys still require no transplants.

"You're doing great," the doctor said.

"This isn't normal, is it?" Ben asked.

"There's nothing normal about your case," the doctor responded.

One more miracle

Several years ago, Buck began putting together material for a book on finances. Then, two years ago, he asked the Lord what to do with all the material he had accumulated. The Lord directed him to put the book on the shelf. Buck complied and set it aside.

"I was scheduled to speak in a church one Sunday and told Ben that I felt the Lord was about to do something with the book I had written," Buck says. "After one of the services, the wife of a church elder walked up to me.

"She said, 'Don't think I'm crazy, but while I was listening to you speak, in my mind I saw you sitting down and writing. You were writing with a quill, and that gave me the impression that it was something you had written a while ago. The Lord's telling me that it's time for you to pick it up again and dust it off.' I looked over at Ben, who had an amazed expression on his face. There was no way this woman could have known about my book."

Buck picked up the book again and began "fine-tuning" it. Then, publishers began asking him if he was interested in publishing with them. He settled on Destiny Image Publishing, and now some well-known people are endorsing the book.

"I never imagined myself as an author," Buck says. "It just happened, and I believe this book is part of some major things that are about to happen in the church."

The book is titled *The Coming Financial Revolution*, and it talks about the revolution in the church as God's people begin to move away from the world's system, especially in the area of finances. Some day, Buck believes, this revolution will provide the money needed for the fulfillment of the Great Commission.

Sign Post

 Walking by faith requires that we put more emphasis on what God is saying to us than what our bodies, or doctors, or lawyers, or anyone else say. We can completely trust in our Lord.

"Therefore I tell you, whatever you ask for in prayer, believe that you have received it, and it will be yours. And when you stand praying, if you hold anything against anyone, forgive him, so that your Father in heaven may forgive you your sins" *(Mark 11:24-25).*

An Investment Gone Bad:

Paul and Janice Triplett

TODAY'S MARKETPLACE is an environment in which fortunes can turn in a day. Investors who suffer major losses may be emotionally devastated.

But if they're Christians, God can transform their losses into learning opportunities, blessings, and a closer walk with Him. It is during times like these that God's sovereignty is manifested in amazing ways, as Paul and Janice Triplett discovered when a downturn in the real estate market wiped out half of their assets.

Like his father, Paul worked as a Realtor® in the San Francisco Bay area, and he and his partners had made a number of good investments. Taking advantage of what they saw as another good investment property, they purchased a vacant shopping center on 10 acres.

True to their expectations, major companies like Wal-Mart and Ford Motor Company, as well as the San Francisco Bay Area Rapid Transit District, showed interest in the site.

"There was a lot of interest," Paul says, "but nothing ever happened. It was costing us roughly a thousand dollars per day to hold the property, and this ended up going on for close to two years."

The time commitment required by the shopping center hindered Paul from making other real estate deals, so his expenses went up as his income went down. And, a slowdown in the real estate market around 1990 made it increasingly difficult for Paul and his partners to sell other properties they had on the market.

Janice and Paul suffered a total loss of about $400,000 and ended up having to sell their house. She called Crown, which set them up with one of the ministry's budget counselors.

The road to financial freedom

Initially, Janice and Paul met weekly with the counselor, who helped them look for a broad range of options for saving money, including cutbacks in Paul's business expenses, changes in their insurance policies, taking lunch to work, canceling all subscriptions, and so on.

"Individually, some of these options didn't look that big," Paul says. "But a couple of dollars per day ends up being a savings of more than $700 at the end of a year.

"We had a debt list that was a page long when we started meeting with our counselor. That list decreased, but Janice kept a growing list of free things that came our way as we were getting out of debt. I won two company trips to Hawaii and two to Mexico. We got luggage, a laptop computer, a cell phone, and tickets to events like concerts and baseball and basketball games. It was unbelievable."

Less encouraging was a letter to Paul and Janice from the IRS, which claimed that they owed $5,000. They disagreed with the agency's finding, but there was little they could do. During this time, Janice found $50 on the floor of a store. She turned it in to the store manager, and someone claimed the money. The next day another letter from the IRS told Janice and Paul that the $5,000 charge had been dropped. Thus, the $50 she turned in to the manager had been multiplied a hundred times.

Better fortunes in real estate

As they continued working their way out of debt, Paul and Janice were able to sell the properties they owned. The last one was an office-retail site that had been on the market for five years.

"We had not had an offer," Paul says. "All of a sudden, within a week, three offers came. We decided to send out a letter giving all three parties one last chance to make their final and best offer. One of them raised their offer by $300,000. It sold and closed on schedule."

Before selling the office-retail site, Paul and Janice began looking for a house to purchase. They had been renting for the past five years.

Finding a bargain wouldn't be easy because the real estate market was heating up and house sellers were receiving multiple offers. One night, Paul and his family put together a list of potential houses they were interested in seeing the following day. Before going to bed, Paul felt that he should check his computer one more time to see if anyone had listed a house at the last minute. They had. "We went out and looked at the house, and it was a good deal," Paul says. "We made an offer, and it was accepted that night."

Because the house had been listed so late at night, other shoppers had already made their list of houses to see the following day and had quit looking for new listings.

Also amazing was the fact that Paul and Janice's offer on the house was accepted even though it was contingent on the closing of the office-retail site that they were in the process of selling.

The contingency required time—something most other house sellers probably did not have. But this particular seller wanted to remain in the house two additional months in order complete two years of residence. As a result, the seller would qualify for a tax exemption.

"We've been in the house for two and one-half years," Paul says. "And in the past five years, my son, daughter, and wife have all completed work on college degrees—with no student loans. The only debt we have is on the house. God has blessed Janice and me in our jobs, and two of the last three years were my best ever in the real estate business.

"My daughter, Elaine, is getting married in July to a Christian guy from our church. She has her real estate license and is going to work with me as a third-generation Realtor®. And our son, Greg, who had worked with Campus Crusade on the campus of UCLA for three years, is now the director of ministry at USC. It's amazing."

The benefits of experience

Paul says that during Janice's and his financial trial, their prayer life increased immensely. They now pray together every day and are teaching Crown small group studies at North Shore Community Church, where he is the Crown church coordinator. When the need arises, they're also doing budget counseling at the church, and Paul is interested in seeing Crown spread beyond his church to fellow Californians in Contra Costa County.

Sharing Crown is rewarding for Paul because he likes to see how the Scriptures quoted in the ministry's small group study change people's lives. Within two years of going through the study, one couple in his church paid off $20,000 in debt. When Paul asked them what they did to turn things around, they responded, "We just stopped buying stuff we didn't need."

From his home in Martinez, California, Paul is not far from Stanford University, one of the nation's most prestigious educational institutions. He notes that a Stanford education can be costly, but it can be cheap when compared to what life teaches us.

"The financial trial we experienced was not something we enjoyed going through," Paul says. "But we wouldn't be teaching and sharing these things with people if we hadn't had that experience."

Sign Post

 Stumbling blocks become stepping stones when life crises are handled according to God's Word. The gate seems narrow sometimes, but the way is always straight.

"I will instruct you and teach you in the way you should go; I will counsel you and watch over you. Do not be like the horse or the mule, which have no understanding but must be controlled by bit and bridle or they will not come to you. Many are the woes of the wicked, but the Lord's unfailing love surrounds the man who trusts in him" (Psalms 32:8-10).

Susan Fontaine Godwin and her husband, Gary.

A New View on Worship:

Susan Fontaine Godwin

SINGING. PRAISING. INSTRUMENTAL MUSIC. We view all of these as forms of worship. Here's another option: financial stewardship.

"Not so," you say. "It's too patterned, too technical."

But as Susan Fontaine Godwin discovered, stewardship is an expression that, like other forms of worship, takes many different forms and comes deep from within the heart.

A musical heritage

Music has long been a part of Susan's life. Before becoming a Christian, she played the guitar and sang in taverns and pubs. She's even done some song writing.

Like other people in the California ski resort town where she lived, she did a variety of things to make a living, including work as a radio disc jockey.

And after giving her life to Christ in a small church in the Sierra Nevada mountains, she played her guitar and sang as part of the church's worship team. Her pastor was musically inclined himself, and the church had a strong emphasis on worship.

In 1984, Susan moved from California to Mobile, Alabama to work for what is now Integrity Incorporated, owner of Integrity Music, which is known for artists like Don Moen, Darlene Zschech, Sheila Walsh, Paul Baloche, and Lincoln Brewster.

Susan, who had a degree in journalism and communications, was working with Integrity's publications department. "We surveyed our readers and found that there was a tremendous interest in worship," Susan says. "So, we launched the first direct mail for Hosanna! Music."

During the years that followed, Susan had a front row seat as the company experienced amazing growth. Its major labels now include Hosanna! Music, Integrity Music, and Vertical Music. It also is a distributor for Hillsong Music of Australia.

Susan remained with Integrity for 11 years before launching her own company, Righteous Oaks Music. Church Copyright Administration, a division of the company, had a growth rate of about 75 percent last year. CCA educates and helps churches and organizations fulfill copyright law requirements by obtaining necessary licenses and permissions to legally use a variety of copyrights.

A new aspect of worship

Given her rich musical background, Susan was confident that she knew a lot about worship. But after going through Crown's small group study, she recognized that there is a link between worship and finances, just as there is between worship and music or worship and praise.

"I've read the Scriptures for years," she says. "They've always been an important part of my life, and I thought I was pretty well versed in them.

"God's Word shows us that our daily lives are acts of worship, but as I saw His view on money, it became clear that how I handle my finances also is an act of worship."

Part of that worship, Susan says, is acknowledging God's ownership of all things. Then, there's the daily task of being faithful with the things, both large and small, that He has entrusted to us.

Remembering the verse, *"Steady plodding brings prosperity,"* Susan says she has to work at being mindful of the small expenses, like lattes, which can add up to $20 per week.

But as she's working on helping herself fulfill what she's learned in the Crown study, she realizes that her current work with CCA is helping churches fulfill some of the same goals.

By seeking to comply with copyright laws, churches make themselves better stewards of the witness God has given them in this world. They also practice honesty by obtaining permission before reproducing copyrights, like making photocopies or rehearsal trax of songs, which ensures that copyright owners receive the payment they are due for their work.

The benefits of God's way

Among the chapters in the Crown study that influenced Susan most was the one on work. In response, she wrote a letter to a former employer seeking his forgiveness for wrong attitudes about her job.

The chapter on debt was powerful for her as well as her husband. "We didn't think we had a lot of debt, and by some standards, we probably didn't," she says. "But we did, and when we really saw the impact of the interest we were paying, we saw firsthand that debt really is slavery."

That was two years ago, and Susan and her husband, Gary, have almost eliminated all of their non-mortgage debt. They're making extra principal payments in order to shorten the life of their mortgage.

"God is so gracious," Susan says. "We took the Crown course in January of 2003, and we had just started building a house. We both looked at each other and said, 'Boy, we wouldn't have done this if we'd taken the course earlier.'

"But we were in the middle of building. So we said, 'Lord, it's your house. You can do whatever you want with it,' and we sought His guidance. The Lord graciously helped us finish building the house, and instead of owing any more money on it we had an extra $2,300 in our construction account when we were done."

The day that Susan and her husband moved into their new house, his primary job was discontinued. Since that time, they've had less money to work with, but they're continuing to take small steps toward paying off their debt. Gary has now joined Susan and the CCA team in helping Christian organizations.

"Somehow—we don't know how—we've made progress toward paying off our debts with less money. God is faithful to us when we take the little steps to fulfill His will for our finances and every other aspect of our lives."

Editor's note: To find out more about Susan's work, visit her Web site, Churchca.com. If you'd like to send her an e-mail, write to susan@churchca.com.

Sign Post

Worshiping in spirit and truth takes the form of things from deep within the heart. It is more than just singing or playing an instrument. It's the life we live. Good stewardship is worship, too.

"Come, let us bow down in worship, let us kneel before the Lord our Maker; for he is our God and we are the people of his pasture, the flock under his care. Today, if you hear his voice, do not harden your hearts as you did at Meribah, as you did that day at Massah in the desert, where your fathers tested and tried me, though they had seen what I did" (Psalms 95:6-9).

A Biblical Perspective:

Tom and Barbara Wiedenbeck

AS SMALL GROUP LEADERS in Wisconsin's capital city, Tom and Barbara Wiedenbeck have taught a broad range of people from varied and sometimes unusual backgrounds.

When asked for a sampling of their students, Barbara replies, "Single parents, retirees, middle-agers, *et cetera*. One older couple was concerned because they wanted to retire soon and their financial house was not wholly in order. One single mom had spent too much of her life in an immoral occupation. But now, she was on track morally and spiritually and wanted to pull things together even more.

"One young couple didn't seem to like each other when they started in the group, due to hard situations they'd been through. Over the course of the study they grasped biblical principles about appreciating your spouse and paid down their debts. They were a different couple by the time the study ended."

The benefits of submission

"For us, the Crown small groups have been sort of a microcosm of the big, broad world that's out there," Barbara says.

However, even though their students have come from a wide variety of backgrounds, the couple have noticed that when those students submit to God, He moves in all their lives in the specific ways that are needed.

"Part of the reason the Crown study is so effective is that it helps people pay attention to God in their personal, detailed, everyday lives," Barbara says. "It is life-changing, and Tom is always impressed with how quickly people's lives are affected. I've also noticed in these studies that God often puts people with similar situations and issues together, and that leads to bonding and support—even in cases in which you might not expect it to happen."

More than finances

One reason Tom continues teaching the study is that he sees its impact on character, not just finances. "Character affects the totality of your life," he says. "The impact of the study filters into people's relationships, workplace, and church life as well as into their checkbooks and credit card statements. It impacts their overall understanding of God and the lives He wants for us."

Another aspect of Crown that Tom enjoys is the friendships he forms with people in small groups.

"As the groups progress, students begin sharing their lives with the leaders," he says. "The leaders can then speak to the hearts of the students without their feeling threatened or defensive."

Raising sheep: Examples from God's Word

Just as they have looked for the working of God in their small groups, Tom and Barbara have done the same on their farm in Oregon, Wisconsin. They moved there three years ago, and Tom operates an electrical contracting business with several employees from this site. Barbara oversees a flock of sheep and one "token" llama.

"Some people buy a Miata or Jag when they hit mid-life," she jokes. "We bought sheep! It is really calming to look out the window and see them there."

But, as Christians, Tom and Barbara also see many of the Bible's object lessons concerning sheep played out before them.

"The Lord talks about shepherding and compares us to sheep," Barbara says. "They aren't the dumbest creatures on earth, but they do some dumb, follow-the-crowd things at times. So, there are scriptural lessons that come to life in our pastures."

"Sometimes sheep are happy with the shepherd and follow directions, going where they are supposed to go," Tom says. "At other times you try to lead or push them to another pasture with better grass, but they keep returning to the same worn-out pasture where they have been.

Pictured (left to right) are new lambs on the couple's Sonsie Farm; pet sheep Robena and Isobel; and Carlo, the farm's "token" llama, age 1.

The Wiedenbeck children: (front row) Grace, (back row) Josh, John, and Joy.

"They struggle and fight the shepherd, even though the shepherd knows what is best for the sheep and even has good things for them right in front of their noses!"

Teaching children to follow God's plan

From the beginning of their marriage 25 years ago, Tom and Barbara listened to Crown's radio programs and studied what the Bible says about money.

They passed on the biblical financial lessons they'd learned to their four children.

"We followed Larry Burkett's guideline of 10-45-45," Barbara says. "Kids should tithe, save half of what's left, and then spend the other half. It's worked very well.

"All our children give above the tithe and have savings accounts. They enjoy serving at church and helping with individuals in need, both here and abroad."

At a time when there is so much negative publicity about young people, the Wiedenbeck children provide an encouraging reminder of what can happen when adults incorporate God's principles, financial and otherwise, into their parenting.

• **Joy**, age 24, graduated with honors from Pensacola Christian College and has assisted with Crown efforts in southern Wisconsin.

She serves in various capacities at church, participates in missions each summer, and sponsors two children through Compassion International, something she has done since high school.

• **Grace**, age 21, works full time at her church's childcare center, the largest in the state, and has her own classroom of toddlers. She sponsors a child through Compassion International and corresponds with a soldier in Afghanistan.

Like her sister, she has served in various capacities at church, and she has a big heart for individuals in need.

• **Joshua**, age 18, has just started college as a criminal justice major. He serves in his church's music ministry, and three days a week during the summer he worked the 4:30 a.m. shift at a restaurant, a job for which he actually volunteered.

He was a camp counselor this summer and sponsors a child through Compassion International.

• **John,** at age 15 and a half, is still home-educated and has been learning skills from his dad this summer.

Like his brother, he serves in his church's music ministry. He has been a camp counselor the past two summers and enjoys working with young children.

"We're entering our 21st year of home education this fall," Barbara says. "We hope our kids have learned some biblical lessons from us or from the outside arenas we've placed them in or encouraged them to pursue.

"We've always felt that the most effective teaching or example is the way you live your life. That says a lot more than whatever we would tell our kids. If what we're living is not what we're telling them, then the words won't make any difference anyway."

Sign Post

 God's Word changes one's character. This effects everything ... and ultimately impacts our finances in a positive way.

"Submit yourselves, then, to God. Resist the devil, and he will flee from you. Come near to God and he will come near to you. Wash your hands, you sinners, and purify your hearts, you double-minded" (James 4:7-8).

Clients Who Cared:

Ken and Elaine Steinbeck

WHEN KEN STEINBECK VISITED CLIENTS of his Nebraska insurance business, he went as an adviser. But time and time again, the people he went to see ended up giving him a little advice of their own.

"My wife and I had been married two years when I got into the insurance business," Ken says. "I worked in an agency for an additional two years. Then, I was promoted to an agency manager position in Aurora, Nebraska, which had a population of about 4,000 people."

There were many strong churches in the town, and a lot of Ken's clients began asking him if he had a church home.

"I didn't have any idea what they were talking about," he says. "I'd grown up in church, but my wife, Elaine, and I had not attended church regularly since we were married."

Eternal life insurance

Ken's clients cared about him and encouraged him to pursue a life of faith. On one occasion, when he was advising a couple,

Pictured (left to right) are Ken and Elaine Steinbeck with their children, Laura and Paul.

the wife had to leave the home. But the husband indicated that he'd like to talk more about life insurance.

Seeing a prospective sale, Ken was happy to grant his request. "He led me back to his office and said, 'I want to talk to you about eternal life insurance,' " Ken recalls. "I said, 'I've heard of universal life and term, but I've never heard of eternal insurance.' Then, we talked about how Christ died for us."

Another client showed concern for Ken's spiritual condition and asked to pray with him. "He did something that has rarely been done with me before or since then, but it was a great comfort," Ken notes. "He said, 'Can I hold your hand while we pray?' "

Although he was a little apprehensive at first, Ken realized the man was genuine, and he was touched and humbled by the prayer.

Who's that on the radio?

Along with the Bible's message on Christian living, Ken was introduced to its message on finances as well.

"As I became more experienced in the insurance world and began doing more business, including financial planning, my clients began telling me about a man named Larry Burkett," Ken says. "I've been amazed at the number of times I've sat at people's kitchen tables and heard them say, 'I heard this through Crown radio a little while back. What do you think?' "

Eventually, Ken asked one of his clients for more information on Crown. The client introduced him to the ministry's radio programs, and he has been a listener ever since.

An example of faith

Evaluating all the loving input from so many clients led Ken to reconsider his need to be involved in church.

He also saw the strength of a particular family in the midst of tragic circumstances and realized the importance of relying on the Lord. The family followed the wheat harvest in Nebraska from May to September and lived in mobile homes with their children for five months of the year.

"I saw them face tragedies like a wrecked combine and a son who was run over by a combine and suffered a broken hip," Ken says. "Yet, they took it calmly. And, whenever I was in their home, I could always hear the local Christian radio station, KROA, in the background. I began to realize these people had something different. They had a calmness and a joy about them. I wanted that for my family."

Through these and other spiritual lessons that kept coming his way, Ken realized he was missing something important by being out of church.

He and Elaine now attend Peace Lutheran Church, a member of the Lutheran Church Missouri Synod.

The fellowship is located in Grand Island, Nebraska, a town of about 50,000 people, where Ken and Elaine live and operate their businesses.

A family trial

In addition to getting involved in church again, another key step that Ken and Elaine took was to follow up on the lessons they'd learned from Crown. They attended a financial training program at their church designed by Ron Blue, now chairman of Crown's board of directors. And, using money from an inheritance they received from his parents, Ken and Elaine paid off their mortgage two years early.

They were considering an expansion of their house because it serves as the office for her business as well as his. But at that point, about a year and a half ago, Elaine was diagnosed with lymphoma. Her treatment involved three months of chemotherapy.

"There were a couple of times when I didn't think she was going to pull through because she was so weak," Ken says. "She had blood clots in her lungs, and she contracted a number of illnesses because her immune system was so weak."

It was in this trying time that the benefits of the changes Ken and Elaine had made were more apparent than ever.

They did not have the financial burden of a mortgage, they had the love and emotional support of a church congregation, and they were seeking the Lord in a way they had not sought Him in the early years of their marriage.

"The cancer experience actually strengthened our marriage and strengthened our faith," Ken says. "We went on our first short-term mission trip in February because we realized God had given us a lot and we needed to give something in return."

Looking back to his first years in the insurance business, Ken is thankful for the clients who expressed concern for his spiritual welfare.

"We're often taught that evangelism is knocking on someone's door," he says, "but sometimes it works the opposite way.

"Sometimes the person who knocks on the door becomes the learner and the person who answers becomes the teacher."

Sign Post

We have eternal life assurance through accepting the broken body and the shed blood of our Lord, Christ Jesus.

"But what does it say? "The word is near you; it is in your mouth and in your heart," that is, the word of faith we are proclaiming: That if you confess with your mouth, "Jesus is Lord," and believe in your heart that God raised him from the dead, you will be saved. For it is with your heart that you believe and are justified, and it is with your mouth that you confess and are saved. As the Scripture says, "Anyone who trusts in him will never be put to shame" (Romans 10:8-11).

Steve Walker and his wife, Esther, who serves with him in the prison ministry

Criminal Justice Home Missions:

Chaplain Steve Walker

FOR TOO MANY PEOPLE THESE DAYS, the prison system is a revolving door. A study by the Bureau of Justice Statistics found that 67 percent of former inmates released from state prisons had committed at least one serious new crime within the following three years.

As a home missions pastor with the Assemblies of God in the 1980s, Steve Walker was aware of this problem and served as a prison ministry volunteer. He had worked three and a half years as a correctional officer, a job that had given him an up-close look at the needs of the prison population.

And, he believed that if inmates were given the opportunity to study God's Word, they would be less likely to become repeat offenders. While praying one day, the Lord showed Steve that he would have an opportunity to put this belief into practice. He was going to become a prison chaplain.

As always, God is not hindered by circumstances, and Steve was chosen from among 63 candidates in 1991 to serve as chaplain at the Bullock Correctional Facility in Union Springs, Alabama.

"I came to Bullock with a sense that we would be doing something different," Steve says. "I knew we would build a chapel here, which we did with the help of several ministries and nonprofit organizations."

Today, at Bullock's Restoration Chapel, inmates can sign up for a broad Bible study curriculum that includes topics like the Holy Spirit, fatherhood, spiritual warfare, and revival and church history. Through the participation and generosity of Liberty Theological Seminary in Houston, Texas, inmates at Bullock can earn college credit as well as a diploma.

The Restoration Chapel building.

The Restoration Chapel curriculum is also designed to teach life skills, and for a long time Steve has offered Crown's financial teaching videos to inmates. He's hoping to expand the curriculum by offering Crown's Career Direct® assessment.

Inmates who sign up for the Restoration Chapel program do so with the understanding that they will be required to work, study, and attend one church service per week.

They receive mentoring from Steve and a strong group of volunteers, and they attend prayer meetings in which they learn how to pray.

Currently, the enrollment at Restoration Chapel is about 150 inmates, some of whom live in a faith-based honor dorm. Steve is opening the program to as many of Bullock's 1,300 inmates as possible.

A concept that works

The early successes of Chuck Colson's Prison Fellowship ministry were an inspiration to Steve. He also knew of inmates who'd been released and hadn't returned to prison because they now had a relationship with the Lord.

In the early 1990s, the state of Alabama had not begun keeping statistics on the success of faith-based programs.

So, Steve began keeping track of graduates from Restoration Chapel. Today, after 14 years of observation, the program has an 86 percent success rate.

And, before the Florida Department of Corrections launched a faith-based program in that state's prisons, it sent a delegation to Alabama to study the work of Restoration Chapel.

"God uses men to accomplish his purposes," Steve says. "But we give all the glory for our success to Him."

A mission field at home

Looking at faith-based programs in prisons throughout the country, Steve is encouraged by the results.

And, he has much to be thankful for in Alabama, where prison officials have added faith-based programs to all of the state's large correctional facilities and to a number of smaller ones.

What's even more amazing, however, is that much of this outreach is being done through the generosity of donors who give financial support as well as equipment. These people have a heart for prison ministry, which Steve refers to as "criminal justice home missions."

Once, while praying, Steve was reminded of Jesus' words, *"Freely ye have received, freely give"* (Matthew 10:8 KJV). He knew his duty was to do his best and trust God for everything else.

"The Lord said to me, 'You will not have any need that I will not meet,' " Steve says. "And, even though it hasn't always been on my time, He has met all my needs for the past 15 years."

Today, Steve is blessed to see elements of the curriculum at Restoration Chapel being included in a faith-based program at Fountain Correctional Facility in Atmore, Alabama, where Crown's teaching videos are also being used.

"I tell folks that if they want to make a difference, find a prison chaplain who has a vision for faith-based programs," Steve says. "Get in there and help him with everything you can. Faith-based programs work because of the power of God. It's hard to beat the Master's plan."

Sign Post

As we do our best to accomplish God's plan in the earth, we can be assured God will do His part.

"But he said to me, 'My grace is sufficient for you, for my power is made perfect in weakness.' Therefore I will boast all the more gladly about my weaknesses, so that Christ's power may rest on me. That is why, for Christ's sake, I delight in weaknesses, in insults, in hardships, in persecutions, in difficulties. For when I am weak, then I am strong" *(2 Corinthians 12:9-10).*

Editor's note: Steve asks fellow believers to pray for the success of Restoration Chapel and other faith-based programs across the nation. To learn more about the work that he and others are doing in Alabama, visit www.alabamaprisonministries.org. If you'd like to send Steve an e-mail, write to chapwalk@ustconline.net.

Crown Financial Ministries

CROWN FINANCIAL MINISTRIES' VISION is to see the followers of Christ in every nation, faithfully living by God's financial principles in every area of their lives. Since 1976, the ministry has taught millions of people worldwide bringing God's help to individuals, families, churches, businesses, educational institutions and governments.

In the mid 1970's while living in central Florida, Larry Burkett (1939-2003) and Howard Dayton, unknown to each other at the time, were separately called by God to search the Scriptures to find out what He said about managing money. Both were personally impacted by the practical truth in God's Word and realized these life-changing principles needed to be shared with other believers. Larry Burkett founded Christian Financial Concepts in 1976 and Howard Dayton founded Crown Ministries in 1985.

Christian Financial Concepts focused on mass media, budget coaching and seminars while Crown Ministries developed a field staff that would train others to lead small group studies taught in the local church. In 2000, Larry invited Howard to be a guest on his live radio broadcast and God then laid it on both men's hearts to merge their respective organizations into one. Shortly thereafter, Crown Financial Ministries was created.

Today, Crown is the largest ministry in the world dedicated to equipping church and marketplace leaders to know, apply, and teach Biblical financial principles. As a nondenominational, evangelical, nonprofit ministry, today Crown reaches millions each year through radio, internet, publishing, seminars, small group studies, catalytic events, and a global dispersed team of staff and volunteers.

For more information about the ministry or Crown, go to Crown.org or call 1-800-722-1976.

Where are you on the map?

You'll notice that this book is a Destination 1 Resource on the Crown Money Map.™ The Crown Money Map™ is a visual guide that shows you a step-by-step plan on how to achieve true financial freedom.

Like any journey, sometimes you'll take two steps forward and one step back. But, the point is to keep trying and don't be discouraged.

To obtain your copy of the Crown Money Map™ and begin your journey, go to CrownMoneyMap.org.